CYBRARIAN EXTRAORDINAIRE

CYBRARIAN EXTRAORDINAIRE

Compelling Information Literacy Instruction

FELICIA A. SMITH

 LIBRARIES UNLIMITED

AN IMPRINT OF ABC-CLIO, LLC
Santa Barbara, California • Denver, Colorado • Oxford, England

Library of Congress Cataloging-in-Publication Data

Smith, Felicia A.
   Cybrarian Extraordinaire : Compelling Information Literacy Instruction / Felicia A. Smith.
       p. cm
   Summary: "This hands-on guide provides a unique compilation of active-learning exercises that will enhance any for-credit library instruction class, no matter what the setting or audience"— Provided by publisher.
   Includes bibliographical references and index.
   ISBN 978-1-59884-605-8 (pbk. : acid-free paper) — ISBN 978-1-59884-606-5 (ebook)
1. Library orientation for college students—United States.   2. Information literacy—Study and teaching.   3. Information retrieval—Study and teaching.   4. Electronic information resource searching—Study and teaching.   5. Interns (Library science)—United States—Case studies.   I. Title.
   Z711.25.C65S65   2011
   025.5'6—dc22   2010051622

ISBN: 978-1-59884-605-8
EISBN: 978-1-59884-606-5

15   14   13   12   11   1   2   3   4   5

This book is also available on the World Wide Web as an eBook.
Visit www.abc-clio.com for details.

Libraries Unlimited
An Imprint of ABC-CLIO, LLC

ABC-CLIO, LLC
130 Cremona Drive, P.O. Box 1911
Santa Barbara, California 93116-1911

This book is printed on acid-free paper (∞)

Manufactured in the United States of America

CONTENTS

ACKNOWLEDGMENTS

I'd like to thank the creators of the Librarian-in-Residence program, Laura Bayard, Dwight King, Margaret Porter, and Andy Boze, and my rotation managers, Thurston Miller, Carole Pilkington, and Sherri Jones. I need to thank everyone I ever worked with at Notre Dame, especially the "Citation Cop" crew. I'd be remiss if I didn't thank the Spectrum Scholars program. My most heartfelt thanks goes to those select few true friends who accept my craziness, and of course to the entire Lanser family, who made this Notre Dame adventure possible.

Last but not least, I'd like to extend a special thanks to my immediate family: specifically, my sisters Karen and Rochelle, my brother Darryl, my nephews DiAndre and Michael, and my father Reverend Robert, and I need to acknowledge my mother, Ola Mae (deceased). Without my family's permission to be different as I grew up, I would not have developed the creativity that has led to my professional success.

As every award speech goes, "I'd like to thank all the little people who helped make this possible. I am forgetting somebody. Anyway, you know who you are. I love you all, and thanks for believing in me!"

1

CYBRARIAN ROADS TO INFORMATION LITERACY INSTRUCTION

Many roads are available for people who choose to help students become information literate. These paths are always a little different, but the outcome is what the person in such a teaching role must become: a cybrarian extraordinaire, as I call it. This chapter will describe various roads to take in preparing to become a cybrarian. It begins with a description of Generation Xers (Gen Xers) and then describes the road to choosing the library and information profession as a career. This chapter also discusses different paths to follow before gaining that MLIS degree.

> My professional motto is "Aliis inserviendo consumer,"
> meaning "Consumed in the service of others."

Many people use the terms *cybrarian* or *cyber-librarian* interchangeably. PCMag. com defines cyber-librarians (the title is often shortened to *cybrarians*) as "librarians who do most of their research and information retrieval via the Internet and other online services." Dictionary.com defines cybrarians—the etymology is *cyber-* ("cybernetics") and *(li)brarian*—as "librarians who use computers and the Internet for their work; any person who works doing online research and information retrieval, especially one who answers reference questions online." Dictionary.com defines *extraordinaire*, from the Latin word *extraordinarius*, as "extraordinary; uncommon; remarkable."

"Cybrarian extraordinaire" is not the only term I've created. "The Pirate Librarian" is my term, and it has begun to be commonplace with the people in my library and university. One of the first questions people inevitably ask is, "Where did 'the Pirate Librarian' come from?" The answer is rooted in one of my first jobs as a Generation X librarian.

Gen X employees typically have been forced to attain the professional skills necessary to build career security in today's skill-oriented yet economically unstable marketplace. Also, Gen Xers often find it necessary to relocate laterally early in their careers to obtain professional marketability and security. For these reasons, traditional concepts of organizational loyalty are foreign concepts to many in Generation X. These people are characterized as possessing a flexible and survival orientation and, consequently, have little difficulty adapting to change. Generally accepted characteristics of Gen Xers include the notion that they are individualistic, technologically proficient digital natives, adaptable and committed to a work/life balance.

Many Gen Xers grew up watching their workaholic parents being downsized or summarily dismissed from long-held jobs. Thus, Gen Xers have what can best be classified as minimal corporate fealty, as evidenced by the ease and frequency with which they change jobs. Gen Xers were typically latchkey kids from single-parent or blended-family households, and this type of childhood contributed to their fiercely independent and intensely self-sufficient personalities.

In the workplace, they value both personal freedom and professional responsibility. Many Gen Xers seemingly exhibit a casual disdain for authority and structured work hours. They tend to abhor being micromanaged and embrace a hands-off management style. It has been said that they "work to live, rather than live to work." Generation Xers often incorporate humor and games into work activities.

While my nature rejects generalized characterizations, the above traits definitely apply to us Generation Xers. For us, the explanation that "we do things this way simply because we've always done it that way" is not acceptable, a hallmark of one of the generational distinctions between more seasoned librarians and newbies.

René Descartes states, "If you would be a real seeker after truth, it is necessary that at least once in your life you doubt, as far as possible, all things." This quote serves cybrarians well as they follow their road, even before they become librarians.

A colleague once told me that the admissions committee for our university's library and information science program was discussing how to recruit the best to the profession. Considering the outstanding students and their backgrounds, one person posed the question "Should we be looking for used car salespersons and bartenders?" Indeed, an outstanding graduate from that program had held those positions before entering the LIS program. This person had a marvelous sense of humor and the ability to sell libraries to the community as well as to serve up desired information.

People interested in a career in library and information science bring their varied backgrounds. My route began when I became a certified criminal-defense private investigator (PI) specializing in homicide and narcotics cases, an occupation my father had correctly determined to be potentially extremely dangerous. His guilt-inducing worrying about me, and a visit to the hospital to see my prematurely born nephew (2 pounds, 4 ounces), helped change my direction.

The librarian in the hospital's new consumer-health library was very helpful with what would happen when my nephew was released to come home. Her ability to help people was very appealing. If I was in the library and the librarian was busy, I'd suggest that a person look at the medical journals while waiting, or even made some suggestions about places they might find what they wanted. My rudimentary referrals were made easier by the way the library was organized. There were teaching models of body parts displayed on top of the shelves, with resources correlating to those issues. For instance, the heart model was atop cardiovascular-related materials, and the brain model was above the books and videos covering neurological issues.

During one of my visits, the librarian was interviewing people for a job. I inquired about the job but was informed that they were interviewing candidates only if they had an MLIS degree. Like many others, this was an unknown degree to me. After an unsuccessful candidate search, the librarian approached me and explained that she had observed the manner in which I took the initiative to help people when she was busy. She stated that she could teach me MeSH (Medical Subject Headings), the U.S. National Library of Medicine's controlled vocabulary used for indexing articles for MEDLINE and PubMed databases.

I was allowed to interview for the job, and the search committee, impressed with my technology proficiency, offered me the job as a health-information specialist if I agreed to get my library degree. A very important reality is that if you sell yourself, you had better be prepared to back it up, even if it includes earning an MLIS degree.

The field of librarianship is an excellent way to use your research ability and to retain the satisfaction of helping people. An academic library was my goal, but in what capacity? The transition into the library profession from the criminal-investigation field was seamless because of my transferable skills. People might wonder why anyone would leave such an exciting job to become a librarian, but amazingly enough, the two jobs are not quite as different as they may appear at first glance: Both require problem-solving skills. Both require information-gathering, evaluation, and authentication skills. Both require attention to detail. An investigator conducts witness interviews with the goal of finding out information the person has, whereas a librarian conducts reference interviews with the goal of finding out what information the person really needs.

Basically, both jobs require effective searching skills. Both jobs require accuracy and a great deal of thought. Both are customer focused. Both demand that you equip yourself with the appropriate tools and knowledge to succeed. An investigator files and locates court documents; librarians file claims for missing serials and locate requested information. Another familiar aspect was being told, "You do not look like an investigator." Many Gen X cybrarians are told that they do not look like a librarian.

PREPROFESSIONAL EXPERIENCES

Some people who choose to become information professionals start off working in a paraprofessional position in a library. The salary for this position may not be equal to a salary one earned earlier. The salary as a health-information specialist, for example, was exactly half of my PI salary. Luckily, though, this job paid for 75 percent of my tuition, and the American Library Association's Spectrum Scholarship paid a considerable amount of the remaining expenses. Earning extra income meant an internship at Northwestern University's Schaffner Library every weeknight, and every weekend found me at the Evergreen Park Public Library. The latter job introduced me to my first library costume, when the children's librarian program highlighted books based on the character Corduroy the bear. The children's librarian convinced me to wear a Corduroy bear suit when the temperature was 90 degrees outside with poor air conditioning inside. The bear suit was only the first of many library costumes and character inventions that were part of my career.

Others have entered library science as a second profession when their first choice disappeared. The profession of engineering, for example, seems to be very vulnerable at a particular time, and then the pendulum swings and engineers return to being essential hires. Other eventual librarians found their first choice not what they thought it would be. In some MLIS programs, a number of students hold law degrees but have chosen to help people find information rather than spend their lives accumulating billable hours. For many others, their technological prowess was a major factor in obtaining a library job. Some of my fellow Spectrum Scholars shared a few interesting stories with me about their prior jobs:

Before becoming a librarian, Kelvin Watson said, he was an infantry officer in the army. "From there, I went to work in book distribution, sales, and marketing at Ingram," Watson added. "After Ingram, I worked for Borders. While there, I decided to go to library school. I am now with the National Agricultural Library in DC."

"I've been a timber cruiser for the National Park Service, and cleaned campground toilets," Nance Acuna Espinosa, now a government documents coordinator, told me. "I was a car hop for Bob's Big Boy, a tax examiner for the IRS. I was a greeter for Gemco: I used to say, 'Thank you for showing your Gemco card' at least 200 times a day. And I was a tree monkey, helping to trim trees."

Pamela Brown said she began as a news reporter and then was a Montessori teacher in grades K–3. Other jobs included teaching in grades 1–4 and substitute teaching. She was also a secretary and a receptionist, a clerk and a data-entry clerk, an assistant broadcast buyer, a traffic manager, a media assistant, and a grant writer.

Joel B. Thornton, who spent seven years as a financial analyst for EDS (formerly known as Electronic Data Systems), is now a CPA.

A librarian with a longer story explained, "Before I worked for the library system, I was a preschool teacher. But before that, I worked at a juvenile detention center. I can't remember my exact title, but I worked with the kids and teens, mainly girls. I had to do initial check-in procedures with them when they were first arrested and also check them for weapons and such before they went into their rooms. I helped supervise them at all times, including school, outdoor time, and meals. It was a scary job sometimes, because I didn't know if they were going to start fighting or acting out. Once, a whole group of them decided to protest something and had to be locked into their rooms for a long period of time.

"I had majored in psychology in college and thought this would be a way to help children with emotional problems. It was much more than that. I left after about nine months because it was too stressful for me. I often took the job home with me in my mind. I did see one of the girls working a job at a movie theater after I left. She seemed happy to see me, and I was happy to see her with a job despite her time in detention.

"I was planning to get my master's in psychology before taking this job. Afterward, I decided to go into teaching at a preschool. Eventually, my path led to the library where I worked, and I got my master's in library and information science with a concentration on youth services. I love my job! I think my experiences there made me see teens a little bit differently, both for the good and not so good. I am attracted to stories about teens involved with the law, like *Monster*, by Walter Dean Myers. I see how teens can be influenced by their environment and home life but at the same time have to make their own choices that may determine their futures."

To further demonstrate the wide variation in prior employment experiences among cybrarians, Marc Levitt, an archivist also in charge of a reading room, said he "managed a retail store that sold table-top strategy war games, metal and plastic figures that one assembles, paints, and then plays a game with on a 3-D board (think of model train terrain) that uses dice and measures distances in inches." Also, he was a fitness coach at Bally's Total Fitness. "Although this was really a sales job," he added, "we had to know all the basics of working out, nutrition, and physiology."

"Before I became a librarian, I worked as a discount-store manager," Mantra Henderson explained. "I saw an opportunity in my local paper for a branch manager of a public library, and applied. Yes, it meant a decrease in pay, but it allowed me to combine my two loves: computers and books. At the time, I did not have my MLIS, but I later on achieved that goal. No, I would not change a thing, because I learned that I made the perfect career choice, as opposed to my original plan of becoming a computer programmer."

Alma Ramos-McDermott said she "spent 21 years as an elementary school teacher before returning to graduate school to get my second master's, this one in library science. I am now a middle school librarian."

G. Salim Mohammed was a financial aid administrator at a major university. "Technically, my job title was assistant director for financial aid—data management and research," he said. "I went back to school and got an MS in geography and an MA in library information studies (back to back at the University of Wisconsin, Madison). My first and current MLS position is as a maps/GIS librarian."

"I was recently laid off from the Queens Borough Public Library due to budget cuts, and I am now a librarian at SUNY Maritime College," Kimmy Szeto said. "Before I became a librarian, I got a job offer as an actuarial analyst at a natural-disasters risk-assessment firm (and turned it down—what was I thinking?). I was a research assistant at a major geological sciences research facility simulating climate and hydrological conditions of the Mediterranean 35 million years ago. I was an arranger and an orchestra conductor for musicals (and lived the life of a freelance musician/arts administrator). I worked as a secretary for a principal at a private K–12 school. I was a math professor at a commercial art and design college, and I was a math professor at a culinary school."

RESIDENT LIBRARIAN

Some MLIS graduates are fortunate enough to find a paid internship or a librarian-in-residence program. These opportunities usually allow them to rotate through different library departments and garner valuable experience so they can make an educated choice about their career path. It helps answer the question "What do I want to be when I grow up?"

A residency gives the new graduate the opportunity to further develop instruction skills. My residency coincided with the explosion of blogs. Blogs are now more commonplace. At that time, libraries were experimenting with launching, hosting, and maintaining blogs to determine whether they can be useful in advancing information-literacy concepts. My residency program provided me an opportunity to initiate other ideas beyond blogging. These are described in the next chapter.

2

RESIDENT LIBRARIAN

When I answer reference questions for patrons I learn things I never knew.
For instance, did you know that licking your own elbow is impossible to do?
Working in the law library was very intense. But it was cool researching famous
    people's nonsense. Such as R. Kelly's alleged child porno offense or lawsuits
    involving, my man, the Artist Formerly Known as Prince.
Next I worked in a chemistry library,
That was understandably scary!
I taught a class for an entire semester, for college credit
I was "Professor Smith!" Who'da ever thunk it?
Now, I'm doing Africana Collection development
Adding materials to ensure my people's history is visibly present.
I've published articles about obscure topics of interest
And been a presenter at a statewide conference
Because as a minority librarian . . . you know . . . I gotta represent!
Working in libraries is challenging but is a lot of fun too
Where else could I work with such an interesting crew?
I work with a Mexican-That-Can, an Indian Princess, and an American King—
    well, technically, two.
I work with a gal on the other side of weird, and the remarkable Miss U.
I work with someone afraid of muffins, and some sort of raptor . . . just to name
    a few.
Librarianship allows me to mine own self be true
Basically, I became a librarian because, to quote Ray Charles, "I'ma make it do
    what it do!"

Felicia Smith

In the next decade, librarians will be in short supply as the number of retirees peaks
and the demographics simultaneously shift to a predominantly nonwhite population.
In response to this issue, the University of Notre Dame's Hesburgh Libraries and the
school's Kresge Law Library partnered to create diversity programming. In 2000,
the initiative, called the Librarian-in-Residence Program, was launched. One place
this librarian-in-residence position was posted was on the Spectrum Scholar e-mail

listserv, which is a good place to find such opportunities. That's where I found out about it, and I was selected as a librarian-in-residence for 2000–2007.

This residency, similar to many others, offers an opportunity to experience various aspects of university research and law libraries. It is a two-year program that allows the successful candidate to be assigned to at least three departments of the university in the first year, with the second year more tailored to the interest of the candidate; time was allocated for conducting a research/writing project as well. Rotating assignments are matched to the resident's technical skills as well as the need to meet the university libraries' strategic goals. The resident also participates in administrative assignments, serves on library committees, is given specialized training, and is offered opportunities for professional activities with travel support. At the end of the residency, the candidate is eligible to apply for a position in the university libraries.

For the first time that year, Notre Dame hired two residents simultaneously. Other universities may have as many as four people simultaneously, depending on the size of the program and the needs of different departments.

The six-month rotations in each department allowed me to audit a class in legal research for first-year law students, teach a course in research skills for sophomore chemistry majors, and create a marketing campaign using a commercial program called RefWorks in the Electronic Resources Department. (RefWorks will be described in more detail later.) During my final rotation, I conducted library instruction and reference services in the reference department.

An interim position such as serving as a resident librarian provides an opportunity to further develop skills learned in the MLS program, especially instructional skills. During this residency, my blog was a way to familiarize myself with blogging technology and to see if a blog could be used effectively in a position as an instructional librarian. This blog attracted a great deal of attention throughout the world from complete strangers who work in the field.

Blogging, in real time or immediately before or after a class, is crucial, allowing the writer to capture the opportunities and challenges of each session. Blogging allows external, like-minded, or shared-interest colleagues to offer suggestions or simple support. Blogging creates a useful archival record of successful class activities or exercises that require further development. If the blog is public, managers may use it to identify areas that are causing their residents to struggle. This chapter reflects the activities noted on that blog and highlights what it takes to be successful as a resident librarian morphing into a cybrarian and someone who must meet the obligations for an academic community. One thing I learned was the adage "If you don't succeed the first time, try, try again!"

NEVER GIVE UP

When three articles I had written were accepted for publication within three months, research and publication could be placed on hold while I initiated other endeavors. While this number of publications in such a short time frame may seem like quite an accomplishment, it didn't reflect all the rejection e-mails, which were very discouraging at times. However, the lesson learned is "Never give up—and never give in!" This can be applied to library instruction. You can have a feeling of dismay when you plan an orientation for international graduate students but only one student shows up and four librarians are there to present. Never give up—and never given in!

THE BIRTH OF AN EXTRAORDINARY CYBRARIAN

Many experiences during the residency contributed to my transformation from being just an ordinary resident librarian to blossoming as an extraordinary cybrarian. In preparing for a final in Legal Research as well as answering an onslaught of reference questions from the first-year law students, one realizes that the cybrarian learns along with students. One quality-control measure of auditing the class required the resident to complete each homework assignment for the following week. The resident was responsible for identifying confusing assignment questions enough ahead of time for the professors to make any needed changes or revisions. Therefore, the resident completed each assignment without the benefit of an accompanying lecture to explain the information being tested on that assignment. In my case, this was also without the benefit of a law degree or a background in legal education.

After lectures, students and resident librarians have the same exposure to class information. Naturally, the students asked questions based on their homework assignments. The students, just like any other library patron, fully expected the answers to be given in a rapid-fire manner, which meant that the resident librarian had to grasp these concepts on a deeper level. This was not one of those times when it was acceptable to respond with "I'll be happy to look into that and get back to you." It was fascinating that the law students would willingly wait for the resident librarian to stumble through the answer instead of ask one of the staff law librarians, because those librarians were also their professors and the students didn't want their professors to know they needed help. It is the same problem all librarians face: Patrons don't want to be a bother or to ask what they consider silly questions, so they are often hesitant to seek help.

The successful resident librarian must be able to move from simply being able to answer those specific questions on weekly assignments to the ability to speak intelligently about subject matter and the overall process and reasoning behind the complex methods. Helping with legal research means serving faculty of the law school just as you would if you were assigned to another branch or subject area on campus. Serving as a resident librarian in this capacity means a steep learning curve that must be navigated quickly. Yet you are at the same time learning the mechanics of teaching, which may be an entirely new experience. It became clear to me why law librarians are required to have a law degree. As a result of the law rotation, one begins to understand and appreciate a great deal about law.

THE TEACHER IS ALSO THE STUDENT

We live, we learn, and sometimes we learn as we go. That was the case with my first for-credit class. Similar to my experience auditing the legal-research class, the upcoming assignments and in-class worksheets for this course were completed without the luxury of having sat through the corresponding lecture. The purpose was the same: to test the assignment in order to identify any needed changes.

One huge difference was the subject matter. This rotation was in the chemistry library. During this rotation, I taught a course, titled Chemical Information Research Skills, for sophomores majoring in chemistry. The challenge here was similar to that of the law class. With no extensive chemistry education background, the students were more schooled in the subject resulting in a higher complexity of questions. Prior to this rotation, the chemistry librarian previewed the class material to facilitate a smooth transition into teaching these classes. The process of pretesting assignments becomes surprisingly easier after an entire semester of practice.

A major factor aside from practice was organization. Developing a system of organizing students' correspondence was key. Printing all e-mail correspondence with students serves as a great reminder and a way of tracking discussions and decisions. Memory overload is a very real possibility when interacting with 21 students, which leaves room for errors or inconsistencies.

GRADING STUDENT ASSIGNMENTS

Grading assignments during the class session is a great way to identify where students are struggling. Immediately returning graded assignments reinforces the information when it is freshest in their minds. In-class assignments are a marvelous way to observe their approach to the assignment depending on whether it involves group work or independent study. What some will find amusing is that after the instructor has toiled all the live-long day, going to painstaking lengths to impart the intricate strategies to search CrossFire, SciFinder Scholar, NCBI (the National Center for Biotechnology Information), and USPTO (the U.S. Patent and Trade Office), among others, there are those students who immediately resort to Google. This, after I have put blood, sweat, and tears into demonstrating advanced search techniques for powerful subscription databases with proprietary information, but these databases are obviously no match for the omnipotent Google.

As a personal touch, motivational quotes were added to each grade sheet when assignments were returned to students. The students' favorite quote was by Mark Twain, who said, "I'm glad I did it, partly because it was worth it, but mostly because I shall never have to do it again." Some residents may share that sentiment after particularly demanding rotations.

One may encounter different complexities with a new rotation. This may be attributed to the fact that during the rotation, you may be physically located in a separate branch library. When you are physically in the main library but your duties are in a branch library, you must figure out which department's supplies, such as photocopier paper and operating cards, should be used.

Residents must decide their grading philosophy. Do you give an A for effort, or do you note a difference between A effort and A work? Is it fair to students who do A work to give similar grades to those who do not? How does one judge " work in regard to searching a database? Sure, there are those examples when drawing a compound structure/reaction in the CrossFire database and then further limiting the results by specifying a Melting Point range and Disassociation Exponent will yield only one result. In that case, it is easier to judge whether the student gets the correct answer or not.

Is it valuable to consider the progress made in comprehension when the students' performance improves from week to week? A counterargument is that some students take advantage of assistance during office hours. Students who review assignments with their instructor will inevitably get the correct answer, which means they'll be evaluated as having done A work. But what about students who attempt it on their own and perhaps miss one step in a five-step process but understood the overall process based on the outcomes, and so on? Grading philosophy is probably not part of most MLIS programs, which is why the residency is so valuable.

TEACHING DATABASES

MLIS programs are very good at teaching students how to use databases that collect data or information stored, typically in electronic format. This is an essential skill for all librarians. Core databases are available for both law and chemistry. Databases may contain either static textual and numerical date or dynamic data and are organized with controlled vocabulary so that information can be sought and retrieved automatically.

When librarians talk about teaching library skills, a large part of that effort means instructing students on the specific search mechanisms of particular resources, including catalogs and databases. Along with controlled vocabulary, most databases have advanced search features, including the use of truncation symbols and wild cards that allow users to retrieve variations of search terms, eliminating the need for multiple searches. Truncation expands a search term to include all forms of a root word, so, for example, "theat?" will retrieve the variations *theater*, *theatre*, and *theatrical*.

A wild card symbol usually replaces a letter or letters within a word, so: "wom*n" retrieves *woman* and *women*. The truncation and wild card symbols vary from database to database. How the symbols are used will also vary. These are four common truncation symbols and wild cards: "!," "?," "*," and "$."

When teaching database searching, it is best to review the Search Tips or Advanced Search Help pages with students, then demonstrate wild card searches to show the differences in the amount and quality of results retrieved both with and without using advanced search options. The results speak for themselves. Furthermore, doing a basic search and then an advanced search in quick succession illustrates the improved quality of results returned after advanced searches.

It is advisable to review the search tips of each database before conducting instruction sessions. This strategy allows the resident-librarian teacher to gain a deeper understanding of how the database functions, and what truncation and wild card options are available.

Another lesson for the budding cybrarian is that it is a good idea to have the students log on to the classroom computers at the beginning of class, as opposed to waiting until after the lecture. This step saved time by letting the computers boot up during the lecture. In one instance, the computer systems took nearly ten minutes to load. To avoid wasting valuable class time when this happened, plan B was used: Screen captures of the entire process for the in-class exercises were used as a contingency plan. Since this was an especially complex database, the visual answers on the screen captures helped reinforce the concepts. These screen captures were uploaded onto the class Web site so students could refer to them as they completed the assignment. Because some students did not have a chance to finish the in-class practice, the screen captures, along with the answer sheets, helped them ensure that they were completing their assignments correctly after they left class. Cybrarians understand that luck favors the prepared.

Another less technical suggestion was to use cover sheets attached to graded assignments. Due to small budgets, supplies were limited, and in an effort to maximize the efficiency of using cover sheets, they were designed to serve multiple purposes, including to provide privacy and conceal the grades on the assignments being returned and to allow inclusion of motivational or humorous quotes as well as interesting tidbits. Chemistry research classes don't lend themselves easily to jokes, so this was a way to sneak in a modicum of levity.

The 30-minute in-class worksheets developed earlier by another instructor were a preferable approach to database-instruction lectures. Good, old-fashioned hands-on practice replaced most of the active-learning exercises I created. However, these exercises can be added as fun activities to the cover sheets when returning graded assignments. While the students didn't have to do the activities unless they wanted to, at least they received them. Feedback on the activities at the end of the semester confirmed that it is a positive solution. Waste not, want not.

TEACHING HINTS

A nice cover sheet should be attached to your graded assignments. You may want to put a typed label with a student name on it on a colored sheet of paper. One popular cover sheet was just a beige blank sheet with the class section number, the student's name, and the Google Scholar/FindText (SFX) Puzzle printed on the sheet. (See Figure 2.1.)

As a part of preparation for each week's class, you should complete the upcoming assignments and in-class exercises and write the grade sheets with comments, attaching answer sheets with correct citations to each assignment. Create a new grade sheet weekly so you can make comments and return their grade with their assignments. Each assignment is different, and so is the grade sheet. Create this on paper first; once the format is finalized, create the electronic sheets.

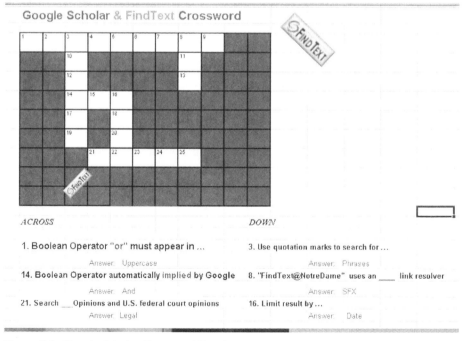

Figure 2.1 Google Scholar Crossword Puzzle

As stated earlier, you may find it helpful to print all the e-mail correspondence with students regarding each day's assignment and attach each student's e-mail replies to that student's assignments. This step will remind you and the student of discussions and decisions that have been made. Interacting with many students requires great organizational skills.

ACTIVE LEARNING

A simple two-minute mini-crossword puzzle was designed to reinforce the nuanced Boolean operators. Google Scholar was the topic, because the students feel at ease with Google. It is important to meet students where they are and gradually bring them along. My suggestion for the way to approach the creation of these activities is really very simple: Make a short list of your goals and potential fun ways to achieve that goal:

1. What is the message I am trying to convey?
   a. Is it simple, or complex?
2. What is the point of the activity?
   a. To introduce material, or to reinforce it?
3. How does the activity allow me to convey the desired message?
4. How long will it take to explain the steps of the activity?
   a. Create printed instructions.
5. Is the activity competing with the message being conveyed?
   a. If a foreign student with no knowledge of this activity participated, would trying to learn the rules of the activity be too confusing?
6. Is it quick, fun, and uncomplicated?

So, what does all that mean? Basically, it comes down to finding the best exercise to reinforce the lesson. For instance, when trying to introduce Boolean operators ("and," "or," and "not") to undergraduates, an exercise is needed that can be completed really quickly. However, if the concept is pretty simple, the students feel a sense of pride at completing the exercise without the benefit of lecture material. Small crossword puzzles make it pretty easy to guess even if they have no prior knowledge. Short word finds or word jumbles work nicely before lectures as well.

Most reinforcement exercises are created for use after the lecture. Exercises that follow lectures work best when teaching a complex concept. Simple exercises following lectures also reveal whether the students were paying attention to the lecture.

Lecture Bingo, one exercise that shows whether they are listening, has words instead of numbers—no more than six words used in the lecture. Create two or three different cards (simply move the first row to different rows on the other cards) and distribute them before the lecture. This way, you can limit the real terms on the card but not have to keep track of a lot of winning combinations. On your notes for class, you can highlight those terms to make sure everyone wins. If you use Microsoft PowerPoint, you can also add animation to those terms as a subtle reminder to yourself. (See Figure 2.2.)

Chemistry students who were not enrolled in the class volunteered to test all the active-learning exercises to make recommendations before they were used in class. It is very practical to have a fresh pair of eyes try activities before administering

LECTURE LINGO

B	I	N	G	O
15	23	37		61
3		40	56	71
14		FREE SPACE	48	69
5	18	41		74
12	27	36	55	65

Every time you hear a word spoken in the lecture,
Place an "X" over the term if it appears on your board,
Until you have five terms in either a vertical, horizontal or diagonal row.

LECTURE LINGO BOARD				
KITTIES	TEACH	GOOGLE SCHOLAR	TWITTER	SEARCH
TOOTIN'	BEACH	CHAT	DANDER	JAZZ
WINE	HOT SAUCE	**FREE SPACE**	OLIVES	EASTER
KARAOKE	COMET	REFWORKS	JEVUS	SPITOON
EMAIL	CATALOG	LOVE	FULL TEXT	FINDTEXT

Figure 2.2 Lecture Bingo Board

them to students, something I learned from being that fresh pair of eyes in my first two residency rotations.

FIRST TIME FOR EVERYTHING: CREATING THE COMMERCIAL

The third rotation included the first exposure to an extended period of library committee and task-group work. It also included my first acting gig—in a RefWorks commercial called "Citation Cop." This parody of the reality television show *Cops* took about five hours of filming, with retakes, to create the final two-minute video commercial after nearly a month of committee meetings. The committee had to agree on a script, create a storyboard, find willing actors and video editors, and get approval from directors in the library and in the Office of Information Technology (OIT), since this was a joint project between the two departments that had purchased RefWorks. The committee agreed that the best format to use is the latest online trend that patrons are excited about, YouTube. Sharing our process provides an example you and your colleagues may wish to follow.

STORYBOARDING

After we obtained permission to use the Office of Information Technology's high-end video camera and editing equipment, designed to edit video commercials, OIT's videographer agreed to help edit. Our responsibility was to create the storyboard, write the commercial script, and line up the actors. The time period for creating this was very short. If you are in a similar short time frame, your process should be similar to ours:

1. Select one script. There is no time for more ideas; you need to pick one and stick with it.
2. Timeline the project and get it on calendars.
3. Recruit actors and schedule times to rehearse and to do the final filming.
4. Identify specifically who will be doing the storyboarding and when it will be completed. A storyboard is a series of illustrations drawn to show the exact sequence of images for the purpose of previsualizing a video or movie.
5. Schedule editing time after completing shooting of the commercial.
6. Upload the commercial video to your library's Web page.
7. Test the YouTube link to the commercial.

Whatever needs to be done should, to be effective, be done with a sense of irony. Think about mocking infomercials. They are easy to make fun of because they are themselves so hokey, but they are memorable, which is what we want. Once we settle on an idea, the next step would be to storyboard it. This is kind of like drawing a comic strip: You have four or six boxes on a regular sheet of paper, and you make drawings in each, perhaps with a caption below each one containing what is being said or what the action of the frame is. Above the box, you list a time code, like two seconds or four seconds. The idea is to time out the scene in a rough way so you know what you want to shoot, who needs to be involved, and so on.

If your video is going to last between one minute and a maximum of three minutes, each shot should have its own frame so that it is clear what the filming needs are ahead of time. You need to add a few shots so the editors have choices from various directions. In developing our video shots, we used frames to show

1. a classroom scene with students and the teacher walking around passing out papers.
2. the teacher handing the student the paper.
3. a shot of the student's expression while holding the paper.
4. a close-up shot of paper with an F written on it.

Extra shots during filming were considered, such as a student being pushed down the hallway to simulate movement. We decided to add two sequences:

1. A student typing feverishly.
2. A close-up of the computer screen to show RefWorks.

The student part of the storyboard had many frames:

1. A student holding a paper with an F written on it.
2. A close-up of the F.
3. A close-up of the student's disappointed face.

The editor has to finalize and approve the storyboard.

This process was new to me. I had never heard of a storyboard before, so it was difficult to know where to begin. Our editor said to use stick figures to sketch out every scene ahead of time so everyone knows the sequence of events. For this, clip art in Microsoft Word and PowerPoint was used, as shown in Figure 2.3.

An updated storyboard was created using PowerPoint. See appendix A for the new version.

Figure 2.3 Storyboard

Citation Cop flashes badge. Cop: OIT Employee	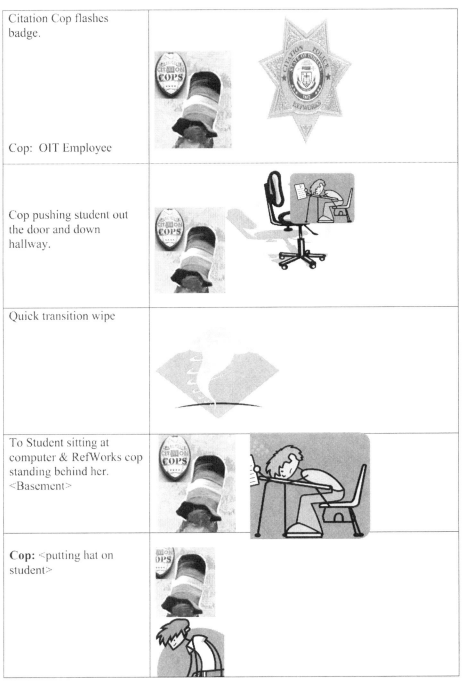
Cop pushing student out the door and down hallway.	
Quick transition wipe	
To Student sitting at computer & RefWorks cop standing behind her. <Basement>	
Cop: <putting hat on student>	

(continued)

Student (Felicia) feverishly types 500 wpm **In her Pajamas** <shot of her front typing>	
<shot of keyboard>	
Student stops typing and takes off hat **Moment of Clarity**	
Quick transition wipe to classroom, <..."The next day...">	
Teacher passing out papers to students. <handing "A" paper to student>	

Figure 2.3 *(continued)*

"A" Student \<looking at camera\>	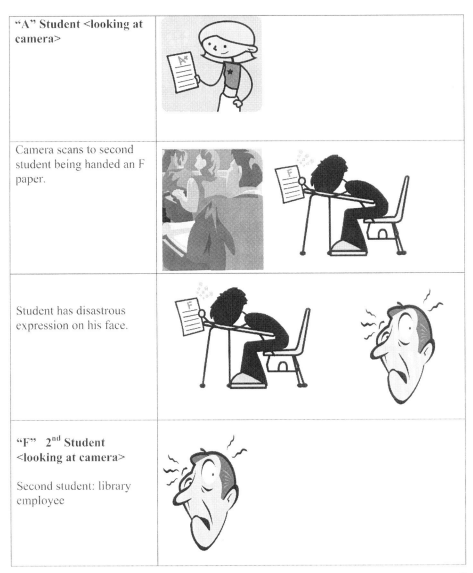
Camera scans to second student being handed an F paper.	
Student has disastrous expression on his face.	
"F" 2nd Student \<looking at camera\> Second student: library employee	

(continued)

<Shot of Cop flying by doorway on chair>	
Cop stops and jerks head towards second student in shock!	
Zooms to Cop's ear	
Advertising final screen **Disclaimer:**	

Figure 2.3 *(continued)*

SCRIPT

I had never taken a drama class, so acting skills were new for me and may be for you. However, the school's film and theater students were gone for the winter break, so the role of the student was my assignment, with someone from OIT playing the opposite role. It was up to me to furnish all the background images, such as a Notre Dame jersey for the student, along with Notre Dame cups, hats, and a wall covering to ensure that, in the minute or two that the video lasts, viewers can easily identify the school.

When the script was finalized, our focus turned to searching for noncopyrighted, royalty-free sound and visual effects, plus props and locations. The character of the student was originally supposed to be filmed atop a flatbed dolly being wheeled down a hall, which promised to be quite the library adventure.

Following is the final script for the "Citation Cop" YouTube commercial:

Narrator:	Due to the graphic nature of "Citation Cops," viewer discretion is advised.
Citation Cop:	Been working the Citation Unit for quite a while now. It's not uncommon for new students to misplace a comma or omit an author.
	(Radio Static Sound)
Dispatcher:	Unit 211, we have a Code 4-1-1 in progress.
	(Radio Static Sound)
Teacher:	(Whispering) I need to see you after class.
Student #1:	(Loud, surprised voice) F? "Incorrect reference format—see style guide"? What does that mean?
Citation Cop:	Excuse me—Citation Police. You're going to have to come with me. You're in violation of submitting a research paper without proper citations.
Student #1:	Ugh! But I was just so confused by all these style guides. I just don't know how to create bibliographies or footnotes!
Citation Cop:	Have you thought about RefWorks? With RefWorks, you don't need these style guides. RefWorks is a powerful Web-based citation tool that does all that work for you. It even creates bibliographies. You'll be citing references in no time. Here, try it out.
Student #1:	(After fast typing, in a happy voice) Whoa! That was fast, Citation Dude!
Citation Cop:	RefWorks, one step from writing to citing!
Teacher:	Good job.
Student #1:	A! Thanks, RefWorks!
Student #2:	F? "No reference cited"?
Citation Cop:	Yeah, citing sources correctly can be messy. But you get by with RefWorks.
	(Radio Static Sound)
Dispatcher:	Unit 211, we have another Code 4-1-1 in progress.
	(Radio Static Sound)
Citation Cop:	One day at a time!
Narrator:	RefWorks is available free on campus at www.library.nd.edu/refworks.
Final Disclaimer Sign:	No students were harmed in the making of this video. RefWorks is brought to you by the University Libraries and the OIT

This was a very funny filming session, and your first attempt may be equally hilarious. Our cameraman fell off the dolly while trying to create the illusion of moving. Some actors didn't run their lines, as they say in the business, which required a few retakes. As shown above, no character in the entire commercial had more than six lines, so there was no real need to study them. As the cast muddled through, one cast member suggested we keep the outtakes and send them to be shown on *America's Funniest Home Videos* or use them in our DVD set as special features.

After we shot the commercial, it went through the editing process. The "Citation Cop" commercial is under two minutes long (1:59, to be exact), so it played on a continuous loop on a projection screen in the lobby. On the day it was shown, librarians were in the lobby distributing freebies as a way to draw patrons to the RefWorks sign-up table. Other librarians were available to help new users create accounts. The video is available on YouTube; to access it, just search for "Citation Cop." This is the funnest job ever! Who says libraries aren't cool?

A few people have expressed interest in using "Citation Cop." After we received multiple requests from external groups, our general counsel lawyers added a Creative Commons license to the original version, allowing licensees to display the work only if they give the author or licensor credit. The RefWorks company showcases "Citation Cop" as a marketing tool for other customers.

THE IMPORTANCE OF COMMITTEES IN ACADEMIC LIBRARIES

To ensure proper time management, the resident librarian may receive a request to create a project-completion timeline. This was the case during my third rotation in the Electronic Resources Department with the library's RefWorks promotional campaign. To do this, it seemed best to create a committee focused on publicity. A challenging part of this kind of project is to convince patrons who don't know they need this that they need it.

Academic-library committees are famously fraught with missed deadlines and often continue to meet for extended periods of time, usually as a result of a noble quest to involve all stakeholders in decision making. However, a resident librarian has a limited time, and one misses deadlines at one's own peril. This initial committee assignment caused more concern when all the members proudly claimed to be contrary-librarians. However, when some suggested that team T-shirts be made printed with our "Contrarians for the Greater Good" slogan, it was easy to see they were also deadline-oriented contrarians.

Groupthink Pitfalls

The general consensus on the RefWorks committee was that humorous videos tend to go viral on YouTube. That was why the "Citation Cop" spoof of the reality show *Cops* was created and posted online. An integral component was the intellectual cohesiveness of the group tasked with promoting the resource. Every group member believed that the librarians' images needed an infusion of levity and fun. While the RefWorks committee worked quickly and effectively, that is not always the case with library committees. Some groups are plagued with obstructionists or, conversely, members who fall victim to a phenomenon called groupthink.

Groupthink is a subtle shift from effective decision making to conformity and an unwillingness to rock the boat. As a result, the team makes low-quality decisions. Groupthink often suppresses individuality. A parable from a real-life experience describes the issues surrounding how individuals reach agreement—or, more specifically, believe they have reached agreement:

> The Parable of the Abilene Paradox: Four adults are sitting on a porch in 104-degree heat in the small town of Coleman, Texas, some 53 miles from Abilene. They are engaging in as little motion as possible, drinking lemonade and watching the fan spin lazily. The characters are a married couple and the wife's parents.
>
> At some point, the wife's father suggests they drive to Abilene to eat at a cafeteria there. The son-in-law thinks this is a crazy idea but doesn't see any

need to upset the applecart, so he goes along with it, as do the two women. They get in their un-air-conditioned Buick and drive through a dust storm to Abilene. They eat a mediocre lunch at the cafeteria and return to Coleman exhausted, hot, and generally unhappy with the experience.

It is not until they return home that it is revealed that none of them really wanted to go to Abilene. They were just going along because they thought the others were eager to go. Naturally, everyone sees this missed opportunity for communication as someone else's problem! (Morse 2009)

As a rule, committees or groups benefit from a moderate amount of both positive and negative member contributions.

Librarians are usually evaluated on service to the profession. Contribution to a professional association is also a critical element for applying for a promotion or tenure. Such committee work is one accepted way to demonstrate professional service. Simply stated, being on a professional committee is very important in academic libraries!

A sample invitation letter offering the opportunity to serve on a professional committee will read, "It is my pleasure, as incoming president of the Association of College and Research Libraries (ACRL), to invite you to serve as a member of the Racial and Ethnic Diversity Committee. . . . Thank you for your interest in and support of ACRL." Professional committee appointments are highly coveted. These positions are hard to obtain because of the large number of applicants for the relatively few vacancies.

During a resident's rotation or in any position where one is doing a variety of jobs, it is difficult getting acclimated to the hierarchy and the acceptable manner to move ideas forward. One needs to be careful of stepping on those toes! Additionally, it is difficult to balance the desire to be involved in numerous endeavors without overcommitting and being stretched too thin.

Making Teaching Interesting and Fun

A successful way to promote library resources is to use the latest online and technological trends or gadgets that patrons are excited about, such as Verbots, Facebook, and podcasts. This was the reasoning behind using YouTube to launch the library's new resource, RefWorks.

One online tool that made instruction fun was on a Web site called Meet Ms. Dewey. The Web site's visual background had a futuristic cityscape, and the site was all in Flash. It was hosted by an animated character students loved named Ms. Dewey, who was preloaded with clever and often cheeky responses to search queries. She seemed like a big fan of Microsoft's hit video game Halo. This was not surprising, since she was an employee of Microsoft. One cool search was "video games," because she not only retrieved information about video games but also started playing one.

The problem with cool online tools is, of course, their fleeting nature. Such is the case with Ms. Dewey. Unfortunately, like so many other cool Web sites before her, the domain name for hers expired in 2009. (There is a Facebook page dedicated to bringing her back.) The program was not available at the time of publication of this book but may return online. As much as the cybrarian in us may love technology, this vanishing act happens far too often.

Verbots

Chatbots found on such Web sites as Verbots.com will also attract students' interest. A chatbot is a computer animation with speech synthesis that understands natural language queries. Chatbots are sometimes also referred to as chatterbots, Web bots, or virtual friends. Users can download chatbot applications free directly from Verbots.com, which boasts that it is the portal to the exciting world of artificial intelligence (AI).

Chatbots allow users to create an engaging virtual personality that can assist with common computer tasks or act as a teacher that can play games or administer tests. Some librarians have reportedly used a chatbot called Sylvie, a sassy young woman with long white hair and a lot of attitude. (See Figure 2.4.) One librarian is said to have set her up on a PC with dual monitors near the reference area to answer basic directional questions. Sylvie can open Windows-based programs, verbally answer questions; or reply to a map request by opening MapQuest.

An interesting development is detailed in an article titled "Use of Verbot Technology to Enhance Classroom Lecture." The article describes yet another Sylvie chatbot; this one is a redhead who was used in instruction. She talks—well, technically, she replies to text-based input by moving her lips in synchronization with an outgoing voice message. Amazingly, she uses facial expressions as a show of emotions. Apparently, this is a simple process. Basically, Sylvie can be programmed using a text editor to give specific responses to users' input. If the name Sylvie is not particularly appealing, there are other chatbots named Julia or Ka.

One chatbot named Stella knows how to handle difficult patrons. She was once asked to remove her clothes, to which she replied asking whether the user is a medical student and whether the user would like to be directed to medical Web sites. The AI trends described here have been helpful in both marketing and information literacy.

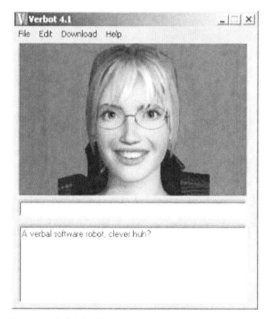

Figure 2.4 Sylvie Verbot

Facebook and Podcasts

It is safe to assume that most students are on Facebook. It makes sense to go where the patrons are; that is why part of library instruction classes includes showing students the library's Facebook search application. It is touted as a way for students to search library resources without leaving Facebook. Unfortunately, our usage statistics show that students have not shown much interest in it. Class evaluations revealed that students view the search application as nice, but they will not add the application to their Facebook page. They went on to explain that they go to Facebook as a way to escape homework and research.

Another seemingly useful trend students use frequently is podcasting. Librarians at Notre Dame spent a great deal of time investigating the possible application of instructional podcasts with a few pilot projects. Unfortunately, they never caught on. For library podcasts to be effective, the purpose must be clear, the medium (podcast) must be a good fit, and it must be determined if it is an audio podcast or a video podcast. It must also be entertaining and, most of all, concise! The overarching critical evaluative lesson here is simple; just because librarians can go somewhere doesn't always mean they should. This rotation in the Electronic Resources Department illustrated that this lesson is especially true with technology.

THE BIRTH OF PIRRRATE TEACHERRR

Q: What is a pirate's favorite animal?

A: An *AARRR*dvark.

Q: What is a pirate's favorite mode of transportation?

A: I guess an *RRRV*.

Q: Wrong! A ship.

The final rotation was in the reference department, conducting instruction sessions and covering the reference service. Once again, it proved to be no ordinary residency. Walking across campus to grab lunch can cause students to come running, asking why you are dressed like a pirate. When they learn it is for a class, they will ask if they can take the class.

The pirate theme began while I prepared to teach a library-instruction class in the first-year-composition program. There were seemingly obvious parallels between the research process of searching for information in databases, in online catalogs, or in the stacks and the scavenging process of hunting for buried treasure. The theme tied together the concepts of pirates looking for hidden treasure with the help of a treasure map and students searching for keywords in a database or a catalog and then locating their booty electronically or physically in the library.

The pirate-themed pilot classes were evaluated to determine which components were considered engaging and which parts were thought to be distracting. The report of the feedback can be found in the article "Pirate-Teacher's Active Learning Exercises," published in the *Journal of Academic Librarianship* in March 2007. Needless to say, the pirate gets a great deal of attention, especially while taking students on a tour of the first three floors of the library. The theme allows teaching about Net piracy and use of pirated materials. The active-learning exercises from prior classes were easily converted to use pirate terminology.

If the pirate costume doesn't grab their attention, the first class activity never fails. The first part of the lecture demonstrates catalog searching by title or keyword. To make the search more challenging, the title is scrambled in a word jumble. The students can solve it directly on their handout, or a volunteer can solve it on the SmartBoard interactive whiteboard's touch screen. To save time, only the first word of the title is scrambled. To save even more time, the scrambled word has only the letters *SAS*. The students have to unscramble the three letters and complete the title, ___ *Is Dead*. The students are much too demure to ever state the answer and may require a gentle reminder that the teacher is a trained professional and can be trusted, even in a pirate costume. Eventually, one brave soul will spell the first word of the title in a soft, questioning voice: "*A-S-S?*" Yes, the teacher replies, the title you all need to search for in the catalog is "*Ass Is Dead.*" (See Figure 2.5.) After the laughter subsides, they are incredibly eager to search the catalog and go retrieve that book to see what it is about.

The students explained how easy it is to participate in the annual International Talk Like a Pirate Day on September 19. To quote a few students, "It was a g*R-RR*eat class!" Instruction was supplemented with the use of the SmartBoard. The pirate-themed and searching-for-buried-treasure-themed activities were successful in breaking up the monotony of lecture-only classes.

THE MECHANICS OF TEACHING

Teaching undergraduates, mainly first-year students, requires an entirely different approach than teaching graduate law students or sophomore chemistry majors. They need more motivation to participate in the learning process during mandatory library classes. One way to accomplish this is to try to make teaching both interesting and fun. Ordinary classes require material preparation and have clearly

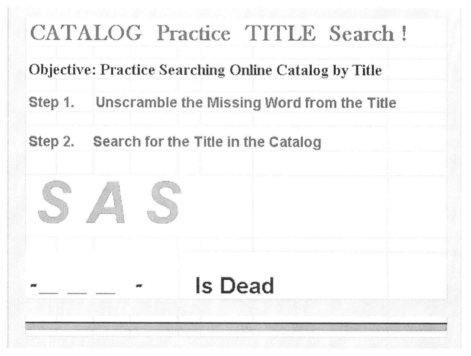

Figure 2.5 *Ass Is Dead* Scramble

stated learning objectives. Extraordinary classes present class material in an engaging manner, thereby exceeding learning objectives by adding a positive association to the subject matter.

For-Credit vs. Orientation Courses

The main difference between for-credit and orientation classes is shown in the expectations the students have. It is understandable that they may be less inclined to focus on library-skills classes during the first month of the semester when they may not have to submit a research paper until the last week of classes. Even if they are attentive, it is highly likely that they will forget the lesson in the coming weeks due to more immediate assignments.

To combat this challenge, it is recommended that the librarian contact the professor before class to identify the current class topics. This strategy allows the librarian to tailor the library instruction to the recent topics covered in the students' classes. One goal of orientation classes is to teach students how to search library resources. But a more realistic goal is often to make them comfortable enough to seek assistance. If all else fails, the students should leave the class knowing how to ask a librarian for help either in person or via chat, phone, e-mail, and so on. Presenting class material in a fun manner goes a long way toward making students less afraid to ask questions and makes librarians more approachable.

Conversely, when preparing for a for-credit course, teaching librarians must fully develop lesson plans for the duration of the class, usually an entire semester. Whenever possible, the homework assignments have to be created and tested. Class lectures and PowerPoint slides should be prepared and timed to ensure that the lecture does not last longer than desired; in most cases, 20 minutes of lecture material is sufficient. It is generally accepted that people's attention spans begin to fade after that amount of time.

Office hours need to be scheduled ahead of time so as to avoid future conflicts. Librarians attend a lot of committee or departmental meetings, so these should be considered when planning office hours. If guest speakers will be invited, they should be given ample time to confirm their availability. Class Web sites need to be created or updated. It should be determined whether online course-management tools such as Blackboard, Angel, or Moodle will be used. As discussed earlier, grading scales must be in place and clearly communicated to the students in their syllabi. Class supplies such as paper for assignments and any teaching materials should be purchased and stored, awaiting use.

Fifteen-Minute Drop-in Sessions

Residents will likely be scheduled to work at the reference desk and to conduct library instruction for a wide range of patrons. Subject librarians teach classes they specialize in, but there are a lot of general public, basic library-skills classes offered to the community that are well suited for residents to teach. During my residency, the library had a few pilot programs offering quick, informal instruction sessions. Though they were scheduled to last only 15 minutes, the drop-in sessions for Notre Dame's online catalog, for online journal articles, and for WorldCat and, of course, RefWorks, these were never well attended. Perhaps there were time conflicts, or perhaps the promotions left something to be desired.

Another type of library-skills instruction for the general public includes programs for students in community groups that are connected to campus such as Upward Bound. Residents have the option to conduct these classes outside of the library building. This is a great way to meet new faculty involved with these programs. It may be challenging to use a different building's technology. After suffering through enough of these technological deaths, one learns how to be reborn through the miracle of low-tech contingency plans and media—otherwise known as paper.

These types of instruction opportunities help residents further develop the much-needed ability to adjust the level of complexity in their classes. Obviously, younger students require activities and lesson plans much different than college students conducting scholarly research.

OUTREACH CLASSES AND WORKSHOPS

Younger audiences enjoy the interactive exercise called Guess the Google at http://grant.robinson.name/projects/guess-the-google/. (See Figure 2.6.) This addictive guessing game based on Google's image search turns the mental activity of searching into a fun and engaging visual game in which people can enjoy the challenge of being the fastest and most efficient at making that connection between search terms and their results. The game requires version 9 or higher of the Flash player to run.

Younger audiences learning basic search techniques really enjoy free online jig-saw puzzles. Many Web sites offer these, but one example is Jigsawsite, at http://www.jigsawsite.com/. (See Figure 2.7.) Just as with the pirate theme, there is a theme when using jigsaw puzzles. The act of solving a puzzle is similar to conduct-ing library searches. When completing a jigsaw puzzle, users have separated pieces that need to be put together in a specific order to reveal a complete picture. The

Figure 2.6 Guess the Google

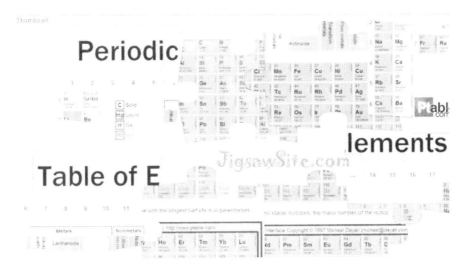

Figure 2.7 Jigsaw

shapes of the puzzle pieces guide the user just like keywords, titles, and author names guide researchers.

If the Upward Bound class is studying the periodic table of the elements, an online jigsaw puzzle can be used as a fast, fun, and focused introductory active-learning exercise before the lecture on searching for science resources in the library. Librarians can quickly and easily create an online jigsaw puzzle from any image on their computer in four simple steps:

1. Click the browse button and select a photo from your computer.
2. Click on the Upload button to upload the photo.
3. Wait a few seconds for the image to be transformed into a jigsaw puzzle.
4. Share the photo jigsaw puzzle with your students.

Younger audiences can especially benefit from the evaluation component of information-literacy standards. Students understandably believe that any Web site with a given keyword in the URL is an unbiased, authoritative, trustworthy source. One particularly effective example of the fallacy of this belief is to show them the Martin Luther King Web site at http://www.martinlutherking.org/. This site, hosted by Stormfront (http://www.stormfront.org/), prominently displays a logo for White Pride World Wide. You must consider the source, no matter how professional a Web site appears.

SMARTBOARD WORKSHOP FOR LIBRARY EMPLOYEES

Residents may be asked to teach workshops for faculty or paraprofessional library employees. One workshop taught the advanced features of the SmartBoard, an interactive whiteboard that allows users to touch the screen instead of using a mouse or a keyboard. One challenge may be keeping the participants' energy level up, especially if instruction is given after lunch. Adding music to some tasks and including a lot of exercises can get your audience out of their seats and using the SmartBoard. Participants should be impressed by its dynamic capabilities.

Participants will likely be interested in the option of using Microsoft Office applications with the SmartBoard; most aren't aware of the built-in recorders and video players. Another crowd pleaser is the beloved spotlight and creative-pen options. The spotlight, which comes in different shapes, such as a circle or a star, allows users to black out the entire screen except for the spotlighted area, while creative-pen options include smiley faces or stars. Whichever pen users select, they can write with that selected image instead of regular fonts. Even though the audience consists of information professionals, humor is still acceptable and appreciated. Library employees typically enjoy poignant cartoons. (See Figures 2.8–2.14.)

All these rotation experiences happen with the knowledge that a resident has only a two-year contract. This means you must pick and choose which professional external activities away from the library you can accept; you may, for example, be asked to present at a conference scheduled after the residency ends. It is vital to use the limited residency wisely, making the best use of your time and travel funds. However, if the request is for a conference with refereed submissions and published proceedings, this offer would be wise to consider.

ACHIEVING CONTINUED EMPLOYMENT

Another wise move for residents is to begin seeking employment at least eight months prior to the residency's expiration. In this economic downturn, it may be best to begin even earlier than that. One major advantage the resident has is the ability to seek employment without the need for covert operations and subterfuge. Making a good impression on all the rotation managers is crucial. These managers usually write an evaluation of the resident at the conclusion of the rotation. Managers can easily

Figure 2.8 Librarian Blues Cartoon Help Wanted

Figure 2.9 Librarian Blues Cartoon Work for Food

Figure 2.10 Librarian Blues Cartoon Out of Order

Figure 2.11 Librarian Blues Cartoon Quiet Please

Figure 2.12 Librarian Blues Cartoon Read All Day

Figure 2.13 Librarian Blues Cartoon

Figure 2.14 Librarian Blues Cartoon Gen X

transfer these into letters of recommendation after the expiration of the residency contract.

The resident should seriously ponder these questions when deciding what type of job would be fulfilling:

1. What interested me in the position/university?
2. What makes me qualified?
3. What is my approach/philosophy to instruction/reference?

4. Do I have good communication skills?
5. Am I innovative/creative?
6. Am I a team player, but am I also able to work independently?

Once the resident answers those basic questions, it is time to search for vacant positions. Many options exist for job seekers. For instance, in 2007, CareerBuilder.com announced that it offers job-matching and internship-matching applications on Facebook. Users can receive continuously updated job and internship listings aligned with the information found in their profiles. CareerBuilder.com offers this service for Facebook users who don't have time to look for a job, and effective job searching takes a lot of time!

Twitter offers services for job seekers as well. Its RSS feed of JobFeed tweets has a 140-character limit that forces concise exchanges of information. Imagine a library job interview conducted entirely on Facebook or Twitter. Not everyone would prefer this type of brief exchange instead of the usual two or three full days of interviews. Certainly, cybrarians should be willing to explore these job-seeking alternatives.

CLOSING

By the end of the residency, one should be able to articulate concrete acquired skills easily and definitively. The resident should be able to compose cover letters detailing specific accomplishments. If the program was successful, the resident will have a much clearer picture of his or her desired career path. Ideally, the resident will be better equipped to answer that pivotal question "What do I want to be when I grow up?"

3

---·•∺•·---

MOVING INTO THE VIRTUAL WORLD: FROM HAVING NO LIFE TO HAVING A SECOND LIFE

A residency is most likely to be successful when your career path is not only clear but also immediately productive. The inherent goal of the residency is for the resident to acquire skills at the sponsoring library to allow him or her to seek gainful employment elsewhere. Fortunately, the first two residents at the University of Notre Dame had both been hired as full-time regular faculty. The year our contract ended, the trend continued: The reference department hired both of the simultaneous residents. This meant a pretty seamless transition as far as expectations because our last rotations were in the reference department.

As part of most academic library departments, librarians are expected to contribute to library instruction. A major difference for me was to set out to revolutionize these classes, which are sometimes considered as less than essential to busy freshman students in their new environments. While developing my pirate concept, I was also researching instructional-technology trends. One example was an awe-inspiring video of the Harvard Law School course CyberOne: Law in the Court of Public Opinion, which incorporated the online multiuser virtual world Second Life (SL) into the class. Recently a fellow American Library Association (ALA) Emerging Leader had mentioned hearing about Second Life, and the search was on to find a creative solution to our Emerging Leader meeting requirements across time zones. In considering the many conferencing technologies, a few of us agreed to experiment with Second Life as an option that would simulate face-to-face meetings. My volunteering to try it was the beginning of Iris Maximus.

For those who may not be familiar with Second Life, the virtual world has nearly 6 million registered users; at any given time, you can expect to find 30,000 people there—virtually of course! For example, in July 2010, 1,383,109 people were logged into Second Life. Its primary use to date has been as a social gathering place, but more and more universities are actively exploring the possibilities of Second Life as an art gallery, library, virtual laboratory, immersive language environment, and more.

In order to test it, one must download the software from http://www.second life.com/. After the software is loaded, users must go through Orientation Island, which has tutorials that explain how to create your avatar, or virtual self, a computer-generated three-dimensional model representation of a person. Users select skin color, height, weight, hair, clothing, and accessories for their avatar. Users can create as many avatars as they want, in any form they want, including animals. Some create personal and professional avatars. My personal avatar looked like Wonder Woman complete with bling—extremely shiny jewelry. My professional avatar for my Notre Dame classes is, naturally, a tiny leprechaun, named Iris Maximus. (IRIS—Information, Research, and Instructional Services—is the official name for our reference department.) Users have to select from a prepopulated list of surnames.

This initial island is where users learn the basics of navigating and communicating in this virtual world. Users can type chat messages or use the voice option to speak to other avatars nearby. To use the voice option, users need a Voice over Internet Protocol (VoIP) headset or a microphone and speakers on their computer. These tutorials also teach arguably the most important function, which is how to make their avatars fly like a bird.

So, after becoming familiar with the basics of Second Life, a few of us from the Emerging Leaders group met on one of ALA's islands. (We had e-mailed our avatar names so we could easily identify each other.) It was instantly clear that Second Life had great potential for library instruction. If you are like me and do not have the programming skills to create the elaborate islands you might imagine, you can just visit other islands that allow users to build objects for free. My usage never got further than 3-D boxes and rectangular tables. Users can copy objects free or purchase items using SL currency called Linden Dollars, which are tied to electronic-payment systems like PayPal. Several online resources allow residents to convert Linden dollars into U.S. dollars and vice versa. Rates fluctuate based on supply and demand, but over the last few years they have remained fairly stable at approximately 250 Linden dollars (L$) to 1 U.S. dollar.

Users quickly pick up the Second Life jargon. SL residents use terms such as "FL," or "first life," and "RL," or "real life," if there is such a thing. When you are in Second Life, you are considered to be "in world." The SL time zone is Pacific Time (PDT or PST, depending on the daylight savings period). This is illusory, however, because when residents are in world, they can change the time of day to night or midday or morning.

While trying to learn how other instructors use Second Life, I was able to view Harvard Law School's video on YouTube. CyberOne: Law in the Court of Public Opinion was the first class at Harvard University to be offered partially in Second Life. The instructors were able to purchase their own island in Second Life because the class was funded by a grant from the school's Provost's Fund for Innovation in Instructional Technology and by the resources of the Harvard Law School and Harvard Extension School, according to a posting at http://cyber.law.harvard.edu/events/luncheon/2006/09/nesson/. (Private islands are actually hosted on private computer servers; when you have a private island, you can choose to restrict access.)

As fate would have it, that same year, our university's Kaneb Center for Teaching & Learning began exploring educational applications of virtual worlds. The Kaneb Center's mission is "to stimulate reflection about—and advocate for the enhancement of—practices, policies, and structures related to teaching and learning." To that end, they created a Virtual Worlds Faculty Learning Community (FLC) to explore the potential of Second Life to enhance student learning. This allowed us to build a series of proof-of-concept projects on our island of Sophia in Second Life. Our private island was purchased with funds from the participating departments represented in the FLC, which also contributed to the annual renewal costs.

As much as it might be helpful to you for me to give you step-by-step details about how to transfer what I see, most of my activities come to me in the middle of the night while I'm sleeping. My colleagues can confirm that most of my e-mails to them for "New Fun Ideas" are sent in the middle of the night. You may work this way, too, but if not, talking with colleagues about how they are making use of new techniques allows you to implement a similar plan in your library.

After I saw that reputable universities were incorporating Second Life, it seemed to me like a good idea to find a way to use it in library instruction. The Kaneb Center was asking for concepts because they were willing to program the ideas submitted by the Faculty Learning Community members. This removed any remaining anxiety and allowed me to come up with innovative ideas for active-learning class exercises. When a literature review failed to reveal any examples of library classes using Second Life, I revisited my aforementioned list questions to apply before creating any class activity:

1. What is the message I am trying to convey?
   a. Is it simple or complex?

2. What is the point of the activity?
   a. To introduce material, or reinforce it?

3. How does the activity allow me to convey the desired message?

4. How long will it take to explain the steps of the activity?
   a. Create printed instructions.

5. Is the activity competing with the message being conveyed?
   a. If a foreign student with no knowledge of this activity participated, would trying to learn the rules of the activity be too confusing?

6. Is it quick, fun, and uncomplicated?

In the case of Second Life activities, what was needed was a simple exercise that would be used after the lectures to reinforce the class material. It is generally accepted that students can absorb up to three new concepts in a given lesson, so concentration was applied to the three creation concepts that were to be reinforced:

First, the difference between scholarly journals and popular magazines.

Second, how to locate books in the stacks and on the shelves.

Third, available services such as Interlibrary Loan and SFX (Find It) options.

The first concept could be achieved by creating a magazine rack divided into two halves: labeled "Scholarly" and "Popular." The rack exercise was designed to reinforce the lecture material explaining how to identify the type of sources. The rack has replicas of magazine and journal covers, hyperlinked to the actual source. The students would then have to move each cover to the appropriate side of the rack. Students eventually received their score on completion.

The last two creation concepts could be achieved by creating a maze. Some of the Faculty Learning Community group attended the annual Second Life convention, which was only 90 miles away in Chicago. At the convention, examples of a multiuser virtual environment (MUVE) maze were on display. (This maze is described in an article titled "MUVEs and Experiential Learning: Some Examples.") The MUVE example was used as the basis, but my maze was different because of different content.

My maze is a series of library tasks or questions about library resources. In the first version, if users answered incorrectly, they were sent to a remedial room and given the chance to answer the same question presented slightly differently, usually with different search terms or different colors. If users answered two questions incorrectly, this told me that they clearly were not paying attention to the lecture a few minutes earlier, so they were automatically kicked out of the maze. Luckily, no one has ever been kicked out unless they wanted to see how it worked. The maze activity was designed as a team or collaborative exercise requiring the entire class to shout out the answers as a way to prevent or minimize incorrect answers. It took a lot of time designing ways that more than one person could be actively involved.

In designing this exercise, it would be inconvenient for each student to have an avatar, mainly because there was insufficient class time to have each student learn how to make and control an avatar. Interested students could take turns as the person controlling the avatar. The controller would select the answer they were given as the result of consensus from the entire class. The Kaneb Center, which eventually created a scoring mechanism that gives students points for every correct answer, helped ensure that my classes incorporated the pedagogical trends toward team-based learning.

Designing your island will be fun and will allow you to be creative. For example, it allowed me to have one thing forbidden in most academic libraries: a kitten. One of the most interesting parts of our planning occurred during the search for a friendly feline for our Second Life library. When searching for kittens in Second Life, one is inevitably lured into sites for sex kittens. This example points out that there is virtual prostitution in Second Life, even though it would be difficult to ascertain how two consenting adult avatars could act out fantasies. Our library cat was chosen and named Snowball, the ND Kitty. Our programmer showed me how to make her meow, which was fascinating. Because I have an RL allergy to cats, having a precious SL kitty is wonderful. All's well that ends well.

The Kaneb Center staff needed to be convinced that a cat belonged in our library. Luckily, there have been a few articles written fondly about felines that inhabit library buildings. One such article described Max the Library Cat, who frequented the Hastings Branch of the Pasadena Public Library. Or perhaps you have heard about Squeakers, the cat-in-residence at Wesleyan College's Willett Memorial Library. Library cats have been around for centuries, and currently greet patrons in almost 150 libraries across the country. Worldwide, 697 cats have been recorded as official library cats.

Once the design and technical, logistical work was completed, Iris Maximus began teleporting students in my library classes for first-year composition students into Second Life so they could navigate through my maze and use the magazine rack. The students definitely worked well as a group on the maze, and there was usually a pretty loud consensus that drowned out any incorrect answers.

In addition to working together as a group, there were a lot of similarities in the Second Life classes. A recurring question in nearly every class was "Can you kill your avatar? This makes one wonder, "If your avatar dies in Second Life, do you die in real life?" Well, since it seems impossible to kill off an avatar, even after many attempts, it would seem we are all safe. The bigger question might be "Why do people instinctively want to kill their avatars?" Ha! That may be too existential.

Students all love to watch Iris dance and are amazed to hear her speak. It was amusing to see that every time a student navigator crashed Iris's avatar into a wall or fell rapidly back to the ground, everyone in the audience involuntarily flinched.

One day, two classes were held back-to-back with the same instructor. The first class really paid close attention to their score. They were cheering on the male student who controlled Iris and chanting "Go, go, go" after he got the correct answer as a way to hurry him when walking through the door. The second class asked if this exercise was timed, so maybe that is why the first class was trying to hurry him along. I told them it is not timed, but the doors don't stay open very long. Also, the first class ended up in the remedial room (on a technicality with the book order), and, when the second class heard about that, they were determined not to go into the remedial room. It was so funny!

None of the students or teachers had ever used Second Life before or even heard of it, so they didn't quite understand the overarching concept of this virtual environment. Even so, the evaluations showed that they all had a positive experience. Second Life classes continue to receive positive comments from both professors and students. These classes allow the use of a new technology the majority of students have yet to learn. Some students request to run through the maze repeatedly because, as they say, "It is fun!" It is refreshing to see that students want to answer library-instruction questions repeatedly. In addition to observed laughter, wonderful feedback on the class evaluation surveys includes the following remarks:

- Interesting.
- Awesome.
- SL seems pretty cool.
- Ha! Ha! Very interesting!
- Cool stuff.
- Fun and entertaining.
- Made class more interesting.
- Really great.
- So-o cool!
- Muy bien.

A few said it was good because it made class more interactive, and 95 percent agreed that "SL is very interesting," though one student out of 80, without any further explanation, reportedly didn't like Second Life.

The FYC professors agreed to let me have ten minutes of class time to take their students into Second Life and get their feedback. Some students said they wanted to spend more time in Second Life and wanted that portion of class to go slower. After the initial evaluations, the Kaneb Center staff agreed to revise some aspects of the maze. For example, some students abhorred being sent to the remedial room when they got an answer wrong, so, because students prefer positive reinforcement, those extra rooms were repurposed into bonus rooms, where students went as a reward for getting the answers correct.

Although the maze is designed to kick them out after two incorrect answers, it is preferable for the instructor to keep this from happening. If they are about to select an incorrect answer, their classmates literally start yelling the correct answer, so expulsions have not been a problem.

After witnessing students' competitive nature, especially in back-to-back classes taught by the same professors, some virtual rewards were added. The Kaneb Center staff added a scoring mechanism to both activities. A heads-up display (HUD) was added that allows users to earn points, and a box was added for students to get their score after completing the magazine rack. (A HUD is any transparent display—basically an eye-level scoreboard—that presents data without requiring users to look away from their usual viewpoints.)

Student evaluations confirmed that they really enjoyed using the magazine rack, moving magazines and journals from the side labeled "Popular" to and from the other side, labeled "Scholarly." This was quick and easy and much more interesting than for me to rattle off a long list of titles and ask about each one, "Is this scholarly?"

Initially, students were allowed to take turns controlling Iris's avatar, but after some complaints that it was boring watching someone else operate the avatar, two avatars were logged in, and students were allowed to take turns on both. This allowed more time actually controlling the avatars, and it showed them how avatars interact and talk to each other as well as do activities together. They really enjoyed racing their avatars through the doors of the maze. In a later revision, to force them to hurry, the Kaneb Center reduced the amount of time the doors stayed open after they answered questions.

Because the laws of physics are nonexistent in Second Life, avatars can usually walk through walls, but Kaneb staff created walls and doors in the maze that avatars could not pass through. After some students said they wanted to get kicked out just to see how it worked, Kaneb staff added emergency exits from each room. This way, students could be asked to complete the activity and then reenter the maze and exit at any time.

A change as a result of student feedback was to the lecture/explanation portions of the class. One student didn't understand the purpose of the exercise. Also, since some class sessions were only 30 minutes long, the explanations about Second Life were rushed. This unfortunate result of running out of time after a 15-minute lecture was explained to future classes. Another comment was that the library building still needed some walls, so it was explained that the programmers were asked not to put in walls.

In a revised lecture, it was stated that, since avatars can fly, there is no reason to take the stairs. Additionally, avatars can fly to different levels, and designers are discouraged from simply creating online Second Life replicas of FL, or RL, physical buildings. During the planning stages, the FLC visited in-world buildings with elevators. This was interesting, but the Notre Dame Second Life library had no elevators or walls, and this was pointed out during the lecture. The students enjoyed seeing that a virtual Touchdown Jesus—a replica of a Notre Dame mural nicknamed "Touchdown Jesus" because of its subject's resemblance to a gesturing football referee—was attached to a Second Life library building even without the wall on which the mural is located in RL.

Another communication challenge was trying to effectively and accurately describe to the students what Second Life is. When first logging in to Second Life, the students get really excited and ask, "What is that? How can we play?" It must be explained that this is not a game, per se.

As with all electronic endeavors, there is the challenge of archiving and preserving your work. When this island is no longer funded, the Kaneb Center needs to capture our work for archival purposes. Making a video or a machinima of the island can do this. (Machinima is the use of real-time three-dimensional graphics rendering engines to generate computer animation.)

Overall, Second Life seems to have one main benefit: You can be who you want to be. This is interesting because most people tend to make their avatars look like themselves. Users have reported that people in wheelchairs have created avatars who are also in wheelchairs, even though they can still fly. In the future, my plan is to have the opportunity to incorporate new technology into classes perhaps in the form of a chatbot, which will allow students to experience a futuristic state-of-the-art technology, intelligent software, and lifelike interaction.

Further plans also include continuing to create interactive educational activities, always with an evaluative component. For instance, it would be good to have students practice searching the online catalog for book titles, then go to our Second Life library to the correct floor to retrieve that book from the stacks. This will train them on the necessary steps for the actual process. One challenge is to provide a seamless process for the students to conduct their online research and then simulate the process in Second Life.

Challenges encountered in the use of Second Life in academia include the following:

1. Finding time for two lives.
2. Justifying taking the energy and time to learn new worlds.
3. Proving the academic benefits.
4. Staying current on changes and new innovations.
5. Obtaining continued funding.
6. Archiving the digital creation and virtual furniture and structures.
7. Safeguarding students. (Only approved users had access initially to our private island.)

HELPING YOUR FELLOW LIBRARIANS WITH SECOND LIFE

In addition to undergraduate classes, workshops can be designed in Second Life for librarians. Your Second Life workshops can begin with a viewing of the *Twilight Zone* episode "Obsolete Man," the tale of a future state where religion and books have been banned. Consequently, a librarian is judged and found to be obsolete by the government's chancellor and ultimately sentenced to death. This episode can make a larger point and provide for extended discussion around the question "Are librarians headed for obsolescence?"

This workshop can be informative and instructive for coworkers. It should be noted that the constant boisterous laughter emanating from these classes may draw complaints from more experienced librarians who fail to understand what on earth a colleague could be doing in these classes either dressed like a pirate or playing video games. It seems logical to assume that an instructor could not possibly be teaching library skills effectively in such an environment. To counteract this perception, my classes are re-created once a year during librarywide in-house training sessions. This sheds a lot of light on what is actually being accomplished in the midst of all the laughing that transpires in these classes. Some librarians may be greatly surprised when they witness that every learning objective listed for these classes has been covered, and yet students have had a good time and have laughed while learning. This in-house training goes a long way in establishing a great appreciation for a different teaching aptitude.

Our Virtual Worlds Faculty Learning Community (FLC) findings can be summarized thusly: The opportunities include collaboration and appeal to students who may already be using virtual worlds for play and interaction. The challenges obviously include taking the time required to create concepts and build the objects virtually. There is a slight learning curve for both faculty and students, depending on their level of engagement. Perhaps the largest challenge, though, is acquiring the technical knowledge needed to write scripts and make the space appealing. The usual hardware, bandwidth, and lag-time challenges are the same that exist with any online venture. Because students are involved in these projects as participants and builders, clearance is needed from general counsel especially because of privacy and security concerns.

As a part of our university's newly created Serious Games Learning Community (LC), we are exploring the use of games in higher education. Our goal is to find or create games designed to improve learning and to implement those games in courses at Notre Dame. Members of this LC include faculty, staff, or students interested in computer games, role-playing, board games, and related pastimes. Our activities will include game play, reading, discussions, and more. Our objectives are to

1. learn what makes up a game.
2. learn how games have been used effectively in higher education.
3. identify and experience serious games in different disciplines.
4. conceptualize a variety of serious games.
5. develop one or more games from scratch.
6. share what we learn, find, and create.

The Second Life planning and design process really helped me fully develop my pirate theme for my other FYC classes. It was a great way to begin my postresidency career as a full-time faculty member.

Following are images of our SL creations, including the maze and magazine rack.

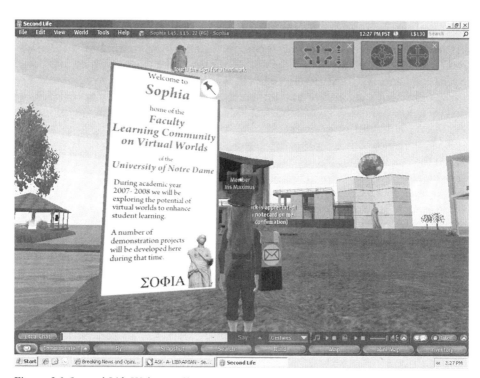

Figure 3.1 Second Life Welcome Sign

Figure 3.2 Second Life Avatar

Figure 3.3 Second Life Kitty

Figure 3.4 Second Life Avatar Picture

Figure 3.5 Second Life Touchdown Jesus

Figure 3.6 Second Life Maze Entry

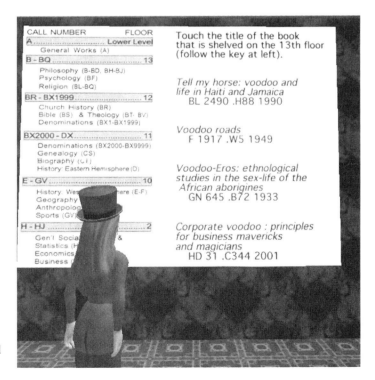

Figure 3.7 Second Life Call Number

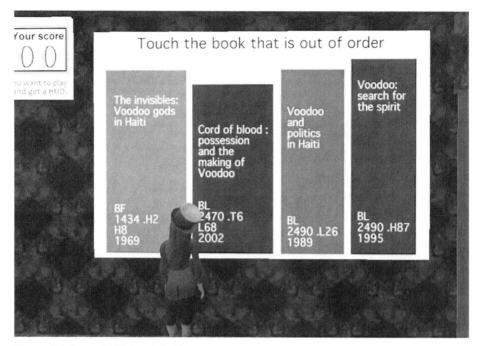

Figure 3.8 Second Life Bookshelf

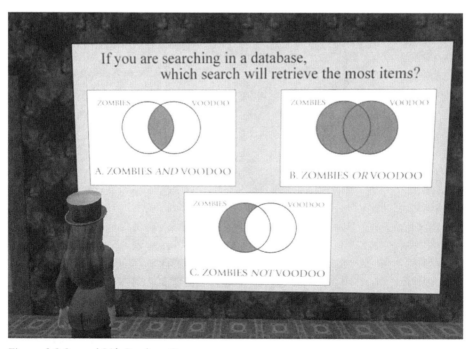

Figure 3.9 Second Life Boolean Ops

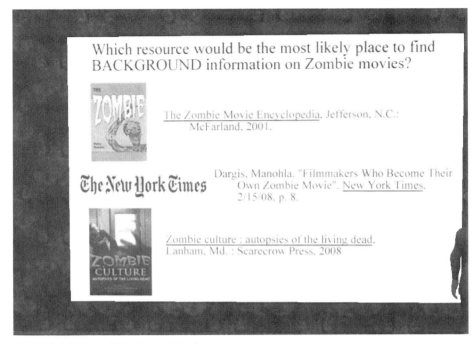

Figure 3.10 Second Life Journal References

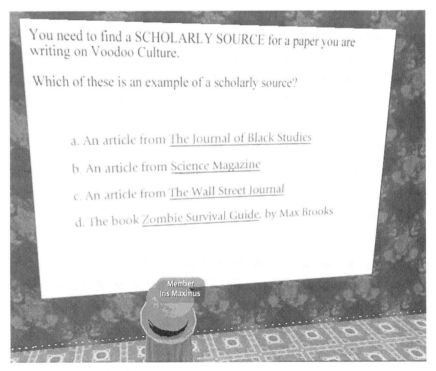

Figure 3.11 Second Life Upstairs

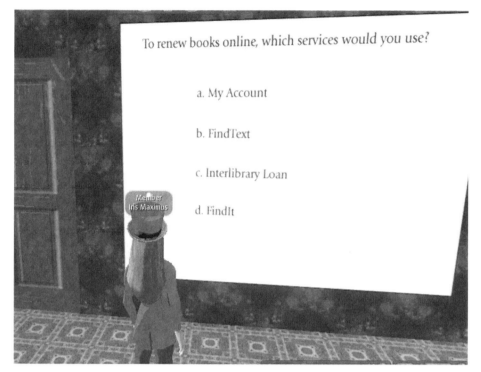

Figure 3.12 Second Life Wall Upstairs

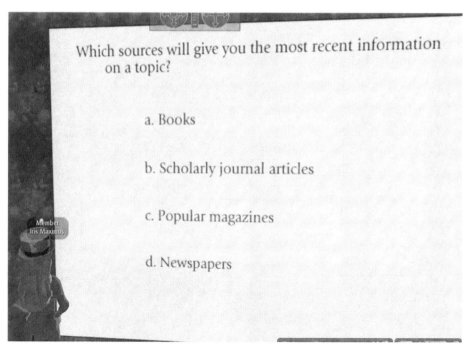

Figure 3.13 Second Life Maze

Figure 3.14 Second Life Rack

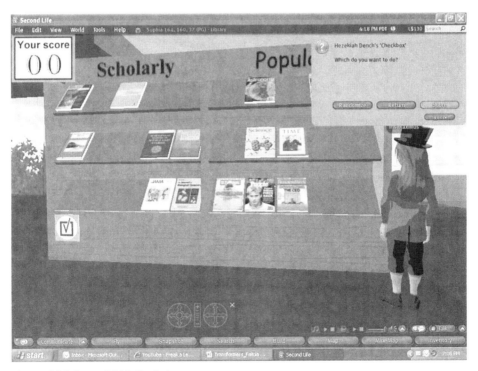

Figure 3.15 Second Life Rack Answers

Not all an academic librarian's efforts are designed to benefit others on the campus. Many librarians are also evaluated for their outreach to their communities. The next chapter shares experiences with the use of the Kindle reading device with teenagers.

4

OUTREACH LIBRARIAN AND WIRELESS READING DEVICES

After my residency, my job title became outreach librarian. The job description included teaching instructional sessions and workshops, developing informational and instructional materials and sessions, and providing reference service to the university community through desk services, personal research-consultation services, and virtual reference. Additionally, duties included participating in marketing and outreach activities aimed at making the library more visible, engaging, and accessible not only to campus and community users but also outside the borders of the university. One phase of this was creating a literacy program at the St. Joseph County Juvenile Justice Center (JJC).

While this was not directly related to my teaching at the university and while wireless reading devices are not yet a part of library life for students at Notre Dame, the possibilities are there. The initial experience came with the JJC program. The JJC director experienced a low-literacy-rate crisis. In June 2008, she expressed a dire need for summer literacy programs at a time when budgetary constraints meant the JJC had to rely on donations and volunteerism.

During the first year's pilot program, the JJC director observed a few sessions. She was so pleased with the initial program that she invited me to come back the next year. It seemed that my presence was a great inspiration to the inmates! They told me what my father the preacher would have been pleased to hear: that my skills included being a motivational speaker.

After the JJC program was featured in the Notre Dame faculty newsletter, other faculty members began discussions on how the JJC program fit with current proposals they were initiating. Some faculty and Office of Information Technology (OIT) members were interested in applying to be one of five universities selected in 2009 by Amazon to participate in a pilot education project using the new Amazon DX wireless electronic reader. So the JJC project led to new working relationships with campus professors and OIT employees. The JJC project also helped accomplish two aspects librarians are evaluated on: university service and community service.

Few students in juvenile facilities are good students or high achievers in schools. They are seldom good readers; therefore, they don't like to read. My task was to reach them and encourage them to begin to read. After I read *The Freedom Writers Diary Teacher's Guide*, one possible approach seemed to be having them read *The Freedom Writers Diary: How a Teacher and 150 Teens Used Writing to Change Themselves and the World around Them*. Reading about the civil rights movement's Freedom Riders inspired the original Freedom Writers themselves. Thus was born the Freedom Readers class for juveniles.

Where and how did this idea come about? This literacy program is rooted in a spirit of service. Motivational speakers encourage their audiences to pursue careers they are passionate about. In my case. it was a passion for criminal justice. Our passions and inspirations compel us to contribute positively to our community. It was also supported by a cybrarian passion: that of using technology. One aspect of this was to change the format of what would be read, and it was hoped that the books could also be offered on a wireless reading device. However, wireless reading devices are expensive, and funds had to be found to implement that part of the plan.

It is highly advisable for both new members and veteran members of academic library staff to take advantage of campus workshops and seminars. One such workshop, Grant Writing, resulted in the writing of a successful proposal titled "Electronic Books Versus Print Books to Improve Literacy at the Juvenile Justice Center." The research purpose of this project proposal was to identify whether juvenile inmates agree that reading electronic books (e-books) displayed on wireless handheld e-book reader devices is more engaging than reading print books. The goal was to implement a literacy program for juvenile inmates to improve their reading and technology skills. The class included the writing and critical-thinking skills as standard information-literacy components. Using e-book reader devices would theoretically provide transferable skills similar to the professional skill set needed to use BlackBerry devices.

The grant detailed the research design, the anticipated number of classes, and the method of data collection. Three groups, each consisting of 14 inmates, would read print books and e-books during six classes. Daily surveys would be used to determine whether an e-book is more engaging than a print version of the same book. Identifying ways to make reading more interesting to this demographic will be useful during curriculum development. At the end of the project, the JJC would receive the final report describing the project's methods and findings, as well as a complimentary Kindle.

Studies of juvenile-inmate literacy and e-books were nonexistent; therefore, this project would introduce a new, nontraditional yet secure approach to literacy (including computer literacy) for correctional facilities. As stated earlier, it is common knowledge that students incarcerated in juvenile correctional facilities have low literacy rates, and there is a widely accepted correlation between low literacy and habitual criminal behavior. The study aimed to address one central question: Would e-book readers increase juvenile inmates' interest in reading? It is equally important, however, to identify material the inmates are inclined to read. Once desirable materials are determined, these can be added to the e-book readers to further increase interest in reading.

The JJC project would serve to determine whether the use of technology (e-books) could be an effective way to increase interest in reading. Ideally, increased interest in reading will lead to improved literacy skills. An added benefit is that e-book readers are not only incredibly portable but also relatively inexpensive and do not violate the JJC's strict security restrictions, which prohibit computer use.

To identify a preferred reading format for juvenile inmates would not only help the JJC's educators develop effective literacy programs but also could be transferred to projects nationwide. As mentioned, studies of juvenile-inmate digital literacy are minimal at best. Studies like the one proposed here, which includes the digital-divide aspect and e-book technology, are nonexistent. This study fills an important void in our understanding and is groundbreaking research. This project's documented success could be reported to and shared with other communities through scholarly publications and presentations.

A simple but productive survey was created. Funds covered the purchase of Amazon's Kindle e-book reader devices and the cost of the download of *The Freedom Writers Diary*. The funds were also used to purchase print versions and class materials such as Sharpies and journals. (Due to security restrictions, inmates cannot use regular ballpoint pens, pencils, or spiral notebooks.)

During the project, a total of 18 classes were held for about 40 inmates housed in three separate pods (dormitories). The inmates were engaged in critical-thinking discussions at least two hours per week pertaining to topics in *The Freedom Writers Diary*. The inmates wrote in journals at least two hours per week.

The inmates used e-book readers during class (at least three hours per week) and were allowed to take personal paperback copies to read after class. This allowed them to test which format is preferable.

The surveys were administered daily. Because inmates in the study changed depending on release or court dates as well as appointments with legal counsel or health care professionals, the surveys needed to include inmates' names. Names were kept confidential. Any technical problems during classes were the researcher's responsibility.

The surveys were administered to all inmates, even those who declined to actually use the Kindle e-book readers. In an effort to ensure that the inmates who used the e-book readers were surveyed, the surveys were to be completed immediately after each inmate had used the e-book readers. This was an attempt to avoid the high probability that the participant is removed from class prior to the end of the survey period. Those who chose not to use the e-book readers or were otherwise unable to use it could complete the survey at the end of class. This allowed those who were not interested in trying the e-book readers to provide feedback and comments as to their reasoning. Waiting until the end of class allowed inmates to change their mind during class, and some were convinced to try the e-readers after watching the positive reactions of classmates.

The juvenile inmates' preexisting attitudes toward reading were the dependent variables in this analysis. The independent variables of interest were preferences shared by age, parental reading habits, and technological access. The survey data was analyzed, and the JJC received a final report describing the findings. This study demonstrated an inexpensive literacy program that can be both technologically relevant and secure from online hazards.

The first year of the Freedom Readers pilot program in the JJC exposed the challenges and complexities of implementing this type of program. The first year's difficulties helped inform the revisions included in the grant proposal. Accounts of that initial endeavor were published in the American Library Association's *Librarians as Community Partners: An Outreach Handbook* as a practical guide for similar initiatives. A report of this study was given at the Continuing Professional Development and Workplace Learning preconference, hosted by the International Federation of Library Associations and Institutions, held in Bologna,

Italy, in August 2009. An extensive presentation on the process and outcomes was given at the National Diversity in Libraries Conference, held at Princeton University in July 2010. (Notes from the class and the survey results are shown in appendix B.)

The most immediate outcome for about 40 juvenile inmates was increased literacy activities. The long-term outcome for the inmates would be greater comfort level with technology. This outcome is particularly important in this correctional-facility population consisting mostly of poverty-stricken ethnic minorities with varying reading abilities and learning styles. This underrepresented demographic was exposed to fun new technology and will hopefully develop more positive associations with reading, writing, and critical thinking.

With the increasing prevalence of computers, most literacy standards now include a technology component. The JJC agreed to permit the use of e-book readers, which allowed some exposure to a new technological device. Ideally, learning to use the e-book readers will provide search-and-scroll skills transferable to devices like the BlackBerry. An increase in literacy programs will lead to more literate inmates who will have a better chance of becoming gainfully employed in an increasingly technologically oriented workforce.

The results of this project, which was both exploratory and descriptive in nature, have special interest to both academic and public library communities. These two groups are wrestling with ways to ensure that reading is not a casualty of the digital age. Incorporating e-book readers may serve as a compromise between old-fashioned professorial ideals (print) and dazzling new options (electronic). It does require careful planning for day-to-day activities, however. (Examples of my daily syllabus and Change Affirmation, the written exercise that had the greatest impact, may be found in appendix C.)

STALL NOTES

As an outreach librarian, I was able to devise nontraditional instructional tools for marketing and instruction. It seems that all librarians struggle with effectively competing for students' attention when students are constantly bombarded by advertisements from a myriad of campus groups and departments. In an effort to ascertain the best way to communicate with students, the librarians conducted focus groups, which unfortunately were not overwhelmingly insightful, though they confirmed that students feel overwhelmed by incessant ads from everywhere. After focus groups with undergraduates, we learned about Stall Notes, posters in the restroom stalls the students really enjoy reading, and they said these are a good source of information. Stall Notes should have funny attention grabbers at the top to allow you to sneak in relevant library information.

Students not only always read the Stall Notes in their dormitories and in the library, they also eagerly anticipate the next iteration. Teachable moments happen everywhere, even in the necessary room. Students have submitted raffle entries using the new Ask-a-Librarian text-message service they read about on the Stall Notes. This is an unusual but good supplemental instruction tool.

Posting Stall Notes in both the men's and women's library restrooms—note: we posted seventy-five the first time—is not for the germ-a-phobic librarian or one with obsessive compulsive disorder, one of my challenges both in my office and at the reference desk. To be effective, one must go into every single bathroom stall at least two times a month to change the Stall Notes. Student assistants could be assigned to post them, especially when a mostly female staff needs to post them in the men's room.

One of the first issues caused a small, unexpected commotion among some people who work in the building because it included references to bathroom etiquette and to personalities from *The Idiot Girls' Action-Adventure Club: True Tales from a Magnificent and Clumsy Life* that are examples of fun reading. Some people took offense to it, inexplicitly. Luckily, however, the majority of my coworkers and managers support the concept and understand that the audience is the undergraduates.

These Stall Notes are hugely successful. One indication in our library was that many of them are stolen by the next day. Sometimes people steal only parts of my Stall Notes. For instance, someone once took only the Stroop Effect color chart and left the rest of the Stall Notes intact. The Stroop Effect experiment is a psychological test that measures people's ability to read words more quickly when they are printed in corresponding colors than when they appear in contradictory colors. For example, if the word *green* is displayed in blue ink, *blue* is printed in yellow, and *yellow* appears in green, test subjects take longer to read the list than when the words are printed in green, blue, and yellow, respectively. John Ridley Stroop first reported this effect in his Ph.D. thesis, published in 1935. Basically, the Stroop Effect chart's goal is to have participants read the words instead of identifying the color they are printed in. (There are plenty of sample color charts on the Internet.)

The other Stall Note that always had pieces stolen included a picture of a turkey looking at a turkey's head on a stick. People repeatedly stole the picture of the turkey, leaving the remaining portion of the Stall Note affixed to the wall. Removing only part of the Stall Note frustrated subsequent readers who tried to figure out what was in the missing picture. This problem required constant replacement because seeing half of a Stall Note is really aggravating and counterproductive. When they do disappear, you may need to decide if you like seeing students walking down the hall with one in their hand to show their friends. It can be flattering to think that they enjoy them so much. (Examples of Stall Notes can be found in appendix D.)

As an outreach librarian, there is for me an inordinate amount of overlap between professional service, contribution to the profession, and community service. Mentoring potential librarians is one example of how one helps the profession grow. Academic librarians in institutions with schools that prepare all types of librarians are in a unique place to help those who are still working on earning their library degrees. Offering mock interviews for people applying for admission to schools of library and information science and for graduating students who are preparing for job interviews can be really helpful. Often, these schools encourage or require a practicum experience, which can also be helpful.

If you are in an academic institution that has a goal of being a premier research institution as well as a goal of creating more visibility for the library, work with departments focused on research. My institution has an Institute for Scholarship in the Liberal Arts as well as a Center for Undergraduate Scholarly Engagement. Others may have special programs for students identified as freshmen with academic potential. As a result of this cooperation, your departments may add an excerpt about the library to their award letters for any scholarships or grants, and they can add information in their newsletters and information packets to raise awareness of subject librarians and special collections. Your goal should be to have the library on your institution's "among the reasons to attend this university" publicity.

Working nights and weekend shifts may be required, but moving beyond scheduled rotations at the reference desk allows you to advertise your availability for research consultations. For those students who claim they are too busy to come to the library, consider creating a mobile reference service called Info 2 Go. Our experiment was to offer services at our student center and in the main classroom building, but it was a limited pilot project with only moderate success. We decided to offer this on-site service the week of midterm exams but didn't take enough planning time or allow time for advance promotions. We sent out e-mails to student listservs and posted table tents in the library, which did not help us with our efforts to show that the library was more than a building.

An outreach librarian is supposed to raise awareness of the services for the academic library's community in general and to raise awareness of liaison services for the faculty in particular. The cybrarian aspect of our profession is constantly changing. All librarians, but particularly outreach librarians, must be vigilant in suggesting effective beneficial uses for new technology designed to help patrons and faculty.

5

---·•·---

PLANNING AND SELLING INSTRUCTION BY THE KISSS PREPARATION METHOD (KEEP IT SIMPLE, SIGNIFICANT, SILLY)

Although you may appear to have less-than-eager students, you should plan to take them on a fantastic voyage through your library's resources. My pirate classes stem from my desire to create a higher level of engagement while maintaining the traditional course objectives, in lieu of a strictly didactic approach to teaching. Reject the temptation to always do things the way they've always been done. Incorporate educational games with predetermined learning objectives into classes. While you may devise active learning exercises that appear to be just fun and games, they can actually be edutainment!

Sharing your active-learning exercises with others will help them improve and may result in publications. The active-learning exercises for a class called Chemical Information Research Skills (for academic credit for sophomore chemistry majors) were shared in an article titled "Games for Teaching Information-Literacy Skills," which has had 1,800 full-text downloads since it was published in 2007.

Incorporate the latest brain-based theories into class design. Active-learning techniques used throughout each class keep students engaged in rather than bored with bibliographic instruction. Professors' and their students' verbal feedback confirmed that this is a more interesting approach to discussing the use of pirated materials than reciting plagiarism and academic-integrity policies. When professors repeatedly request your classes and recommend them to colleagues, it is further proof that a creative approach to library instruction is effective and highly desirable.

You will need to get the students' attention first. One way I do so is to ask them to gather in front of the library. While I in no way approve of violence, I arrive in my pirate's costume and sneak up behind an unsuspecting student, stabbing this student with my collapsible sword. As the blade retracts, it lets out a loud scream and lights flash bright red. In all the times I've been doing this, not once has any classmate who sees me approaching warned my victim that some weird lady in a pirate costume is walking up to him or her with a sword drawn. This simple introduction at the entrance to the library gets huge laughs followed by competing frantic requests to use the sword.

When students come to the library for instruction, make full use of your Smart-Board. You can ask them to write one of their silly nicknames on the SmartBoard using their fingers as pens. This produces a lot of comments like "Wow!" from students who have never used a SmartBoard. Their nicknames elicit a chorus of laughs among classmates as they are asked for explanations of really silly nicknames. Design your classes to allow these moments of levity at the outset of the class as a way to put students at ease. This clearly sets the tone for the entire class, reassuring them that this required library-use class is not going to bore them. They can sense that this is no ordinary class.

While demonstrating how to search the catalog or databases, you can ask for search terms or titles. However, students may not have a quick answer or a good one for the demonstration. It is better to already have a chosen title provided by the professor ahead of time. This allows you to maintain control of the flow and pace of instruction and allows students to breathe a sigh of relief because you aren't relying on them to produce search terms under duress.

To further strengthen the relationship with faculty, you can offer syllabus enhancement by recommending resources adjacent to their assignments as listed on their syllabus. Ideally, this will raise awareness of resources and help alleviate potential student frustration in locating library material. It makes perfect sense to identify the best resources for students at the same time they receive their assignment. This streamlines their research efforts, and it simplifies the assignment process. You may wish to post a promotional statement on your faculty's Web sites. Here is mine for you to adopt or adapt:

> The goals of an assignment often include students learning how to choose the right online database to find sources. At other times, that's not an issue, and you'd prefer they go directly to the best tool and get to work. When the latter is the case, you need to know which product is the most appropriate. There are a lot to choose from, and you may not have the time to do the legwork. Felicia Smith at the Hesburgh Library can help. She wants Notre Dame faculty and TAs to know that your librarians stand ready to offer a set of electronic resources tailored to any specific activity. If you will e-mail Felicia your syllabus or the description of an assignment or project, she will contact the appropriate subject specialists. They will provide you a set of recommendations that you can incorporate into the syllabus or share with students in class.

If you should create a video using the model of "Citation Cop," you can show it to all your classes, both undergraduates and graduates. A short, simple video is significant when it shows a librarian in a humorous way while providing an overview of a valued resource in an interesting and attention-grabbing manner. Following are examples of other simple yet significant games, such as word jumbles, word finds, and crossword puzzles, that I add to classes to break the monotony of lectures.

Word jumbles are one simple activity that can make search-technique demonstrations more engaging. (See Figure 5.1.) The only preparation is to scramble the search term, either a keyword or an author's name. It is best to use the author's name if it is funny or the same as the professor's name. This can be created very quickly and is something most students instinctively know how to do.

Word finds are easy to create using Microsoft Excel by formatting the spreadsheet to display the grid. (See Figure 5.2.) Using tables in Microsoft Word can help you create word finds just as easily. Simply fill in the search terms, then save that as

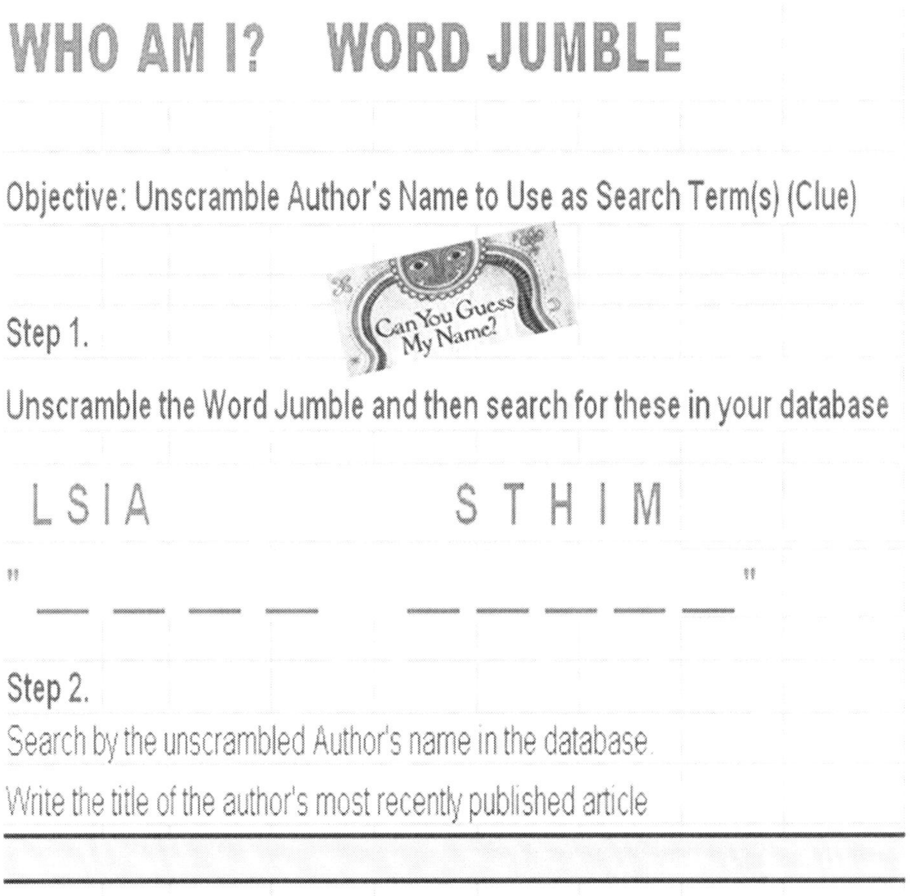

WHO AM I? WORD JUMBLE

Objective: Unscramble Author's Name to Use as Search Term(s) (Clue)

Step 1.

Can You Guess My Name?

Unscramble the Word Jumble and then search for these in your database

L S I A   S T H I M

" ____ ____ ____ ____   ____ ____ ____ ____ "

Step 2.

Search by the unscrambled Author's name in the database.

Write the title of the author's most recently published article

Figure 5.1 Who Am I Word Jumble

the answer sheet. The only thing left to do is fill in the remaining squares. Depending on how long you want this activity to last, you can make the entire grid or table very small, only a few rows and columns, or very long. Another way to make this more complex and time consuming is to fill in the remaining squares with words that resemble the real search terms. If you want to make it go faster, you can fill in the remaining squares with a lot of qs or zs.

If the objective is to introduce truncation or Boolean operators, crossword puzzles are uncomplicated options. (See Figure 5.3.) You just create a connected series of squares and link the terms the way they would appear in a crossword puzzle. Number the squares going across and down. Write the hints at the bottom of the page under lists labeled "Across" or "Down." Then, shade in the remaining squares. This is, again, something that should not require a lot of preparation or explanation but provides mental stimulation.

In preparing for classes, try to include an "Aha!" portion for each session. Include an introduction of a cool resource such as Google SMS or Google Language searches.

Because high tech tools can disappear without warning, you will appreciate low tech equipment as a part of a contingency plan needed with any planning process,

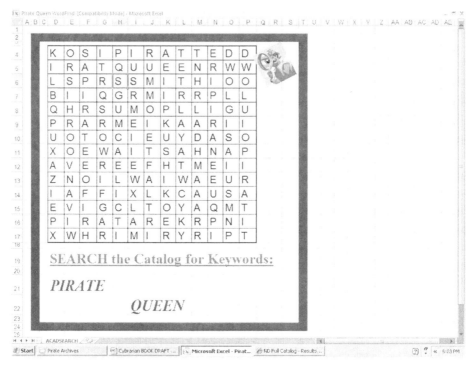

Figure 5.2 Pirate Queen Word Find

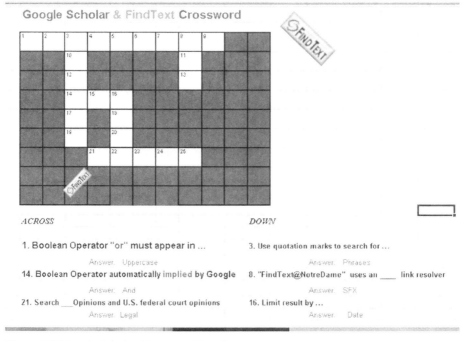

Figure 5.3 Google Scholar Crossword Puzzle

simple or otherwise. What works one time in one classroom may not work another time in an adjacent classroom. Have a backup plan for any planned use of technology that might and often will fail.

Probably the most often-occurring problem is with real-time use of databases. You may wish to have backup Microsoft PowerPoint screen captures with images of what students would have seen had you been able to continue with the use of a balky online database. This takes a little time in the preparation of your lecture, but it pays off when you lose the online database.

The main focus of your class preparation involves putting yourself in the seat in which your students sit. You should plan and then practice the class as you have outlined it. This will allow you to time it exactly. If you record your rehearsal, you can review and then identify good times for breaks in the lecture and add exercises to get students involved and moving toward the SmartBoard. One incentive comes with the length of the class. If you confirm with professors that you are able to dismiss the class at the completion of your instruction (early), then, if there is a lull in participation, you can mention that the sooner the class is finished, the sooner they can leave. This will never fail to get them back on target!

One of our main goals as academic librarians is to create independent learners who can efficiently locate, critically evaluate, and effectively use different formats of information to garner accurate knowledge that can empower them to transform their lives and the world. We strive to create information-seeking specialists with refined skills capable of battling the legions of misinformation mongers currently handicapping society. Information-literate students are more likely to be successful academically, and they will be empowered to transfer literacy skills into all aspects of their lives—personal, professional, and sociopolitical. They need to have information for their lives, not just for homework. They need to become independent learners who can find and reflect critically on information in all fields and formats.

Another important goal for our instruction is conversion: teaching learners to transform mere data into information and to integrate acquired information into knowledge to empower themselves and to improve society. Students need to have a thirst for the most precise information from the most reliable source in all aspects of life, thus making themselves lifelong knowledge seekers. Because learning can transpire anywhere, it is a good practice to venture out of the library and instruct students in their classrooms.

LEAVING THE LIBRARY FOR THE CLASSROOM

Plan to take your instruction performance on the road. When your original plan is to offer a session in the library and this has limited success, sharpen your sales pitch to secure an invitation to the classroom. Visit professors' classes and teach short instruction sessions on site. These classroom visits allow you to target your instruction objectives to actual assignments. This point-of-need instruction is more beneficial than library classes not directly tied to specific, immediate assignments.

Maximum interest comes with offering to visit a professor's classroom, promising to use only 5 or 10 minutes of their class time. Requesting a longer amount of time will find most professors politely declining due to their perceived time constraints. Usually, however, when you request just 5 minutes of class time, you will be offered more time to speak to their students. Make sure you preview the class syllabus so you can use relevant searches during your instruction. It is vital that instruction is as targeted and meaningful as possible.

Some teaching theories encourage instructors to maintain a brief silence after they ask questions during class, which allows students time to reflect prior to answering. These pregnant pauses may not work in the professor's classroom, however, especially if time is limited. Unfortunately, when you are visiting a classroom and only have 10 or 15 minutes at your disposal, time is of the essence. Therefore, use this opportunity to further lighten the mood and get a quick chuckle from the students. Before every class, get the syllabus and ask the professor for a list of subject terms or titles that would be relevant to that day's lecture.

Asking students to volunteer to give answers or suggestions will inevitably generate awkward pauses in class. If you do have a volunteer (perhaps one with an unusable answer), thank the volunteer and state something like "That is a great answer" and proceed with the search with a better term. The chuckles from the students should indicate their approval of your preparedness. This allows you to maintain control of the class and, at the same time, alleviates pressure from the students.

Providing students with instruction in finding resources has always been a challenge. This can be somewhat alleviated by the use of educational games.

SAMPLE EDUCATIONAL GAMES

Many active-learning theorists encourage instructors to provide rewards or prizes that serve as a motivation. This new generation of students is characterized as having low thresholds for boredom; therefore, interaction, group activities, and levity have become essential pedagogical practices. Science has determined that people process information using their dominant side of the brain: Left-brain scholastic activities focus on logical thinking, while right-brained activities focus on creativity.

Traditional instruction methods usually favor left-brain modes of thinking. While active-learning models encourage increased usage of the right brain, that is not to the exclusion of the left brain. This suggested creative approach to instruction allows you, essentially, to get twice the brain. Ample evidence is available to show that lengthy lectures are ineffective, especially for the new generation of learners. The antiquated one-way stand-and-deliver, you-will-listen-to-me approach is not very engaging. The onus has always been on instructors to spark student enthusiasm for learning, as opposed to being dismissive of their painfully obvious boredom, and that is even truer today.

Awarding small, silly prizes is another way to infuse humor and a little something extra into each class. Freebies can be any item with the library's logo or contact information on it, such as badge holders (lanyards), pens and Post-it notes. Amazingly, students are pleased to receive library magnets, pens, and the like as prizes. Other inexpensive, store-bought prizes work well, too. A trip to the Dollar Store, for example, provided one of the funniest prizes: miniature toy cars. These allowed for an amateurish imitation of Oprah Winfrey's car giveaway, when she randomly pointed at audience members during an episode of her television program, exclaiming, "You get a car! You get a car!" followed by the climatic declaration, "Everybody gets a car!" A few weeks later, one student said he still played with his toy car, and others said they really loved the pens. The fact that these students recalled their library-instruction class weeks and months later illustrates that these actions are indeed simple but highly effective!

In addition and as often as possible, humor should be incorporated into classes. This can take the form of funny quotes, cartoons, or jokes. If you are not comfortable with being a public speaker, project something on the screen as students are coming into the class. Yes, the latest YouTube sensation works. There is nothing more attention grabbing for students entering a dark library classroom than to walk in and see a video of a dancing banana singing "Peanut Butter Jelly Time" or seeing the skateboarding dog or the famous dramatic hamster turning around in his dramatic fashion.

Regardless of how you provide instruction, you must evaluate your classes. This will help you determine any changes you can make that may increase both student interest and student learning. Evaluation is covered in chapter 6.

6

————•◦•————

EVALUATING YOUR COURSES

In many institutions, evaluating courses is required. In others, it is an option. Even if formal evaluation is not required, you need to find out as much about your teaching as you can through informal assessment.

When course evaluation is required, you may choose to use the university's standardized teacher- and course-evaluation (TCE) form as your formal assessment tool. Most of these have written responses as well as scales to check. Often, these evaluations do not exactly fit what a cybrarian teaches because they are more aligned with full-semester courses taught by subject-area professors. However, most universities have staff in their testing departments who can help you devise tests for your classes.

The written responses from my students revealed that my activities were highly regarded, which shows that a different approach is highly acceptable to them. When your overarching goals are to both enhance the curriculum and convince faculty your classes are worthwhile, your evaluation will tell them to what extent this was achieved. You can always use variations of your evaluations with other classes.

When results from my first 100 pirate-class evaluations revealed that 86 percent of students agreed that the activities were engaging and were not distracting and 95 percent agreed that the activities were preferable to a lecture-only format, I realized this was a good approach. Activities were derived directly from lecture material to augment but not replace class lectures. Clear objectives were explicitly expressed, tested, and achieved. Your activities should be purposefully simple, and neither time-consuming nor distracting. They should keep students interested in the lessons. Students appreciate taking a break from the monotony of lectures. You must become a reflective practitioner, observing the students' body language to see if they are exhibiting a high interest level. When it is not, you need a plan B or even plans C and D to change the pace. A good written comment from my evaluation was "An otherwise boring and painful course was not so boring and painful!" No matter what we try to convey, if students aren't listening, instructors are not being effective! And when students report that they don't understand the purpose of a session, you may be rushing the explanation to meet the time allocation for your instruction. When this happens, you must alter your beginning lecture so you can explain it in future classes.

Informal evaluation can be used to test to see which method is best. This need not always be done with a formal university evaluation assessment tool. You can devise your own. When you devise your own test and administer it, you need not report the results to anyone. What you are finding out is what you need to do so you can make improvements in your planning and teaching. If you need help with informal assessment, the university's testing department can help you with that, too.

Much more detailed research was conducted for the outreach program in the St. Joseph County Juvenile Justice Center (JJC) when I taught there. This was done because the granting institution required a report of the results. If you are going to initiate a different way of conducting your program, you may wish to consider the process with a much more formal way of evaluating your courses. The example that follows is from the research design followed for the project proposal.

While survey questions for the students were purposely simplified, the following hypotheses were created:

Hypothesis 1. E-book readers loaded with books students like to read will significantly increase inmates' interest in reading.

The conventional wisdom is that this entire generation may be more inclined to prefer reading digital or electronic text than older generations do. Interactive books for young readers bring a new level of synergy between words. These books promote interaction at a new level of intensity between book and reader and often abandon linear and sequential progression.

As with inmates and e-books, you might wish to test whether library instruction/ orientation in Second Life might appeal to more students than a lecture with activities. You would need two groups of students, and you would teach them using both methods.

Hypothesis 2. An inmate population is a victim of the digital divide.

The main premise of the concept of the digital divide is that lack of access to technology disproportionately and negatively impacts lower-income people. Many inmates are from the lower socioeconomic levels in society. A logical conclusion suggests that poverty-stricken people are more likely to be disadvantaged when it comes to access to technology.

Most college students are from higher socioeconomic levels in society, but they may still be disadvantaged because they attended high schools with poor library services. While students who come to college are well acquainted with cell phones and many forms of social networking, they are unaware of the resources they will find in their libraries. A simple survey early in the first session could determine the level of experience your students bring from their basic education experiences. If inmates are not interested in technology, they may be less interested in e-books. If university students are less interested in technology, they may not be interested in participating in a Second Life session.

Hypothesis 3. Personal characteristics are more significant predictors of preferences after independent variables have been taken into account.

Individual characteristics may be more significant predictors of preferences after controlling for other relevant factors such as of age and technological access. It is a common belief that parental reading habits have an impact on children's reading patterns. An individual's experiences and personal background will produce significant differences in preferences, and an example of personal background is a preexisting affinity for reading or a dislike for reading. Students in correctional institutions may have difficulty reading or may have a learning disability, which means they won't be interested in reading in either format. These reasons will hopefully be illuminated in the open-ended questions.

Students who have had less-than-pleasant experiences throughout their school years may be very disinterested in what could be offered in their academic library. These will be the students who arrive late, sit as far away from the front as possible, and have an attitude that dares you to make anything interesting to them.

The juvenile inmates' preexisting attitudes toward reading were the dependent variables in this analysis. The independent variables of interest were preferences shared by age, parental reading habits, and technological access. Testing your students for their preexisting attitudes towards seeking information in a library could be your dependent variable. Your independent variables could be the amount of technology available in their high school and their knowledge and use of social networking.

While an immediate outcome for the juvenile inmates was increased literacy activities, the long-term outcome, hopefully, was that these students would have a greater comfort level with technology. It was not possible to test this in the JJC, and you may not be able to test the long-term success of your teaching. Part of the challenge here is to determine if faculty are giving assignments that would lead your students back to the library to find information.

Finally, the results of this JJC project were of special interest to the academic and library communities as outcomes for ways to ensure that reading is not a casualty of the digital age. Incorporating e-book readers may serve as a compromise between old-fashioned professorial ideals (print) and new dazzling options (electronic).

One of my most effective forms of evaluation has been my blog and the journal I kept. Here are two examples from my first year's journal and two from the time after we had the Kindles:

(YEAR ONE)

Day One—Boys' A Pod

I loved it. Only 3 or 4 students were removed by the correctional officer. I just happened to bring six extra syllabi and six extra books and pens (Sharpies), so that was perfect. I had exactly 21 students. They were incredibly participatory. There was only one nonblack student sitting with the black students. He defended da bruthas against the white boys who expressed confusion over using the "N" word. I plan to do the activity tomorrow to get them to desegregate themselves.

I opened instantly with Les Brown's *Live Your Dreams*, using a powerful delivery to grab their attention. I used intense eye contact with each student. Vicki the director LOVED IT! The students said I should be a motivational speaker or a teacher. The majority agreed that I should be a preacher! I laughed out loud, explaining to them that my daddy would be pleased to hear that. But there were some comments that may have been intended to be flattering that were actually disrespectful, like being told, "She bangin'—she got it goin' on" as I was eyeballed up and down, which forced me to immediately put an end to that. I was mentally prepared to maintain a fun but respectful atmosphere. I decided I was not coming there to get any of them into more trouble, but I instantly, explicitly stated that I would not tolerate any flirtatious comments directed at me. One tiny kid who was the youngest by far, only 11 years old, was clinging to me and drew a lot of teasing from the older boys. After putting a quick end to the flirting, I next set down the class ground rules so everyone was clear about what was acceptable. I explained that I need all of them to participate in my discussions, and so I need people to feel comfortable participating, without negative comments and teasing.

Phew! So, after that was done, I asked, "Who likes to read?" They all said they do. So I asked the ones who wanted to read aloud to sit in the front of the circle we made with our chairs. I explained that the only person allowed to read (talk) was the one holding the special yellow Sharpie. I needed to find a use for the yellow Sharpie, which was not useful to write in their journals with because it was hard to see. Some call this the wagon-wheel technique. One boy admitted he likes to read but he can't read well. I asked the class if they had any suggestions for him. I was pleasantly surprised when the others encouraged him by explaining you just have to practice and said they would help him. And they did. I realized early on that they are all very opinionated and they all want to share those opinions. So, tomorrow's Take a Stand activity promises to be interesting.

They get unbelievably excited about passing out stuff. I had one boy hand out the books, another distributed the Sharpies, and yet another handed out the journals. The last student handed out my syllabi. I had to agree to let different boys collect the pens at the end of class because one was so upset that he didn't get a chance to help.

I am most proud of my flexibility. Anyone who knows me knows that I need structure. All of my control flew out the window literally five minutes into my class. Students were removed to go to court or meet with counselors or parole officers. UGH! The first volunteer to read literally opened the book and was removed to go to another meeting. Alrighty, then. Breathe—"Who else wants to volunteer?" While that student was reading, students were coming and going constantly. The entire class was like that, but I was proud of my ability to just keep it moving!

Day Two—Boys' A Pod

Vicki called me right before I arrived to ask me about the discussion on race we had yesterday. Apparently, the conversation spilled over into another class and the teacher expressed a great deal of concern. Vicki, who is incredibly supportive of my program and who recommended this book, explained the policies and politics of the corrections department. She suggested that it would be easier to continue this program if I simply avoid discussing topics including race, sexism, gangs, and drugs. She had heard about my class discussion about Snoop Dogg's CD cover, which is a cartoon but is sexist. I explained to her that we were reading the book and the book talks about the CD cover. When she stopped by my class today, I showed her the excerpt in the book. I reassured her that I have a lesson plan and gave her my syllabus showing the discussion topics. I explained that I never leave without bringing the discussions to a positive conclusion. I e-mailed her a copy of my revised syllabus literally 13 minutes after I returned to work. I was relieved when she replied that I was doing a great job and the students love my class.

See, I am able to teach using a book written by gang members who use drugs and are sexually active without discussing gangs, sex, or drugs. Good grief.

A few students got released today. One boy sat in the back of class literally crying and praying.

Luckily, they loved the Take a Stand activity. Even the two correctional officers assigned to my class sat inside of my discussion group, and they got just as heated as the students. I was not sure how to handle this, because at one point a boy yelled at the guard that this was their class and he should not be invading their discussion. I held my breath; I think the boy had a point, and I wanted them to participate, but I think he may have been joking because the discussion did not miss a beat. I know I have to walk a fine line because if the guards don't like me, they can make my class a lot more difficult than it already is. The discussion was so successful that I ran out of the planned topics and had to make up more on the fly. The students were clamoring for the next topic. Ugh . . . umm . . . OK. I made up some equally interesting points for debate. I can't even recall them. but they worked.

During my *Soul Train* version of "Hokey Pokey," I instructed them to lick their own elbow. Two of my more clever students licked their fingers and then touched their elbow. Ha! Ha! Funny. But they correctly pointed out that I did not say they couldn't use their fingers to do it. OK, so they won that round. This made me reflect on the first two days, and I have to admit that I was shocked to find that these boys are not dumb by any stretch of the imagination. I was worried about trying to find a happy medium to accommodate kids from 11 to 17 years old with different reading skills. But I actually ended up having to increase the level of difficulty on some activities to keep them engaged and challenged.

YEAR TWO ***ADDED THE KINDLES***

Day One—Boys' B Pod

I have 12 students; 2 were in my JJC class last summer. So, while they were happy to see me, and excited about the new format of the class using the Kindles, I was disappointed and stunned that they were back. Only 1 student did not want to read using the Kindle. No one was removed from my class.

Since I received the Kindles a few minutes before my class, I didn't realize that the page numbers are completely different. And depending on the size of the font, the pages differ.

All of the boys who used the Kindle loved it, especially the fact that definitions appear at the bottom when you place your cursor in front of a word.

I didn't have time to get a student worker to help me with my JJC class. I wanted to have a student worker who could show the JJC students how to use the Kindle while I taught the class. The one who didn't try it said he felt stupid because he "don't" know how to use electronic stuff. So I found time while the other boys were writing to show him individually how to use it. He loved it and actually showed me how to do something I didn't know how to do on the Kindle. I told him how proud I was of him. That is what this class is all about: teaching technical skills, no matter how small.

I was caught off guard by the students actually yelling to be able to read. Since I only had 7, they had to share. I constantly heard shouts of "I want to read next." "Nope, it is my turn to read!"

Every librarian's fantasy has to be a classroom of kids fighting to read!

When I heard that an inmate had choked one of the guards right before I arrived, I didn't want a fight to break out in the class. I created a more organized system to guarantee them that everyone would get a chance to use the Kindle.

Eleven out of 12 preferred to use the Kindles. The one student I worked with individually said he didn't know how to read so he did not want to read on either one, even though he thought the Kindle was cool and like a laptop.

Day Two—Boy's B Pod

Five new students today; four inmates liked the Kindle but one survey showed one preferred print.

When I told them to jump to a different chapter, one of the boys freaked out because he hadn't read that far ahead and was afraid I was going to ruin the ending. I told him it is not really that kind of book and I am not going to go to the very end. I told him I jump around the book based on the discussion topics and themes.

Following are tabulations of the responses to the Kindle Survey, Year Two:

e-Book Reader (Kindle) Survey YEAR # Two: *56 Total Respondents*

Age?

12 = 1   13 = 1   14 = 8   # Answered the question = 56
15 = 11   16 = 13   17 = 19   18 = 3

Grade in school?

N/A = 5   6th = 1   7th = 2
8th = 1   Freshman = 12   # Answered this question = 56
Sophomore = 15   Junior = 12
Senior = 8

Do you prefer reading using the e-book reader?

                                      # Answered this question = 56

Yes = 46   No = 10

Do you prefer reading the paper book?

                                      # Answered this question = 56
Yes = 23   No = 33

Would you be MORE INTERESTED in reading if using the e-book?

                                      # Answered this question = 56

Yes = 44   No = 10

Do you like using the e-book?

Yes = 50   **No = 6**

Answered this question = 56

What specifically do you like *or dislike* about the e-book?

Answered this question = 56

Like = ☺
This is a sample of some responses:
 Like a lil laptop
 Smaller and won't need to mess with pages
 Size and ability to store books
 It's electronic
 Easy to read (also, easier to see words or can see words better)
 Can press the buttons to turn the pages
 Definitions

———————————————

Dislike = ☹
Many fewer responses such as "might drop and break," "like paperback better."

———————————————

Do you or someone in your home own a laptop or computer?

Answered this question = 56

Yes = 46   **No = 10**

How often do you use a laptop/computer?

Answered this question =
 **Only 54 answered

Daily = 32 Weekly = 15
Monthly = 3 Other = 4

Highest level of school completed by parent/guardian: Mother

High School = 15 Some College = 13 Graduated College = 19 Other = 7 (Written additions = Middle school, No school, None; 2 = GED)

Answered this question =
 **Only 54 answered

Highest level of school completed by parent/guardian: Father

High School = 22 Some College = 11 Graduated College = 6 Other = 5 (Written additions = No school, None, Marines)

Answered this question =
 **Only 44 answered

Did you see your parents reading?

Yes = 46　　　　　　No = 10

Answered this question = 56

If yes, how often?

Always = 11　Often = 18
Sometimes = 17　Not at all = 3

Answered this question =
　**Only 49 answered

Do you like to read?

Yes = 46　　　　　　No = 10

Answered this question = 56

If yes, how often?

Always = 17　Often = 14
Sometimes = 15　Not at all = 1

**Only 47 answered

If yes, what do you like to read?

Comics = 9　MySpace = 25
Magazine = 10　Other = 31
(Written additions included Blogs,
Bible = (2), Novels, This book or
books (5), Everything = (4),
Adventure, Autobiographies,
Mysteries = (2), Action = (3),
Love stories, Romantic Books,
Fiction/Novels = (3), Realistic
Books, War Books

*** Final (Overall) Kindle 2009 surveys ***

23 Total Respondents in 2009 for Final Day Overall Survey

Did you participate in all of the class activities?

23 = Yes　　　　　0 = No

** Multiple Answers Per
Student**

Do you like to read more as a result of this class?

18 = Yes　　　　　5 = No

Do you like to write more as a result of this class?

21 = Yes　　　　　2 = No

Do you like to discuss topics with people with different viewpoints more as a result of this class?

20 = Yes　　　　　3 = No

Whether you follow university procedures and administer their instructor course evaluations or create your own, you must evaluate your teaching. You need something concrete to tell you when you were successful and when you need to make changes. Don't dismiss the idea of asking the university's testing department to help you, especially if you are designing a very formal study for a proposal application or for research you wish to do and then report in the literature. Cybrarians with new ideas need to implement and then test them and then report those successful teaching activities in the literature for others to be able to implement, too.

7

SHARING THE PRESENT,
PREPARING FOR THE FUTURE

Once you have captured faculty and students' attention, you have to keep it. Unfortunately, any creative endeavors, even the pirate routine, get old after a time, not to mention that it is exhausting being a pirate. Changing in and out of costume can take ten minutes, which is a lot for just a 30-minute class. People inevitably ask what the future holds for the pirate cybrarian. When one tries to predict the future, reflecting on the past can often provide insight. Based on past extraordinary experiences, the cybrarian will probably continue looking for parallels between experiences that are unalike and try to find commonality that can be used creatively in a novel manner. Certainly, sharing the present with as wide an audience as possible is a good start to preparing for the future.

In the past, harnessing creative forces led to achieving the requirements of professional academic librarianship, specifically by conducting instructional sessions and contributing to scholarship. The future promises to be a continuation of these accomplishments, but in a more focused manner. Past achievements have led to more opportunities. Networking at professional conferences can lead to opportunities such as membership on editorial boards.

As an editor reviewing manuscripts, it becomes clear to me how important original concepts are in the selection process. Approaching the profession in a unique way can attract attention and result in interesting articles, videos, and classes. Unconventional methods have been shared to reach captive audiences in restrooms, and larger audiences through presentations and publications.

In one article, "J.A.W.S.," parallels are drawn between completely unrelated topics. This article frames the challenges of rising subscription costs by comparing this unsustainable situation to the movie *Jaws*. Using excerpts from the movie, the story of a great white shark, the story is rewritten so that it takes place not on and offshore from Amity Island, but inside a library. The article contains a revised movie script that illustrates the parallels between the terrorized islanders in the original movie and the tormented librarians warring against rising subscription prices. Librarians take the place of the weary islanders who are menaced by an ominous force that grows stronger every day. Publishers of scholarly journals take the place of the great white shark, or the villain who is threatening but not willfully evil.

Due to the graphic nature and adult language used in the scripts, reader discretion is advised. The revision illustrates parallels by excerpting some of the most notable quotations from *Jaws* for the library version. The following movie characters have been replaced in the J.A.W.S. analogy:

- The tourists in *Jaws* are the library patrons in "J.A.W.S."
- The shark in *Jaws* is the predatory scholarly-publishing industry in "J.A.W.S."
- Captain Quint, Chief Brody, and Hooper in Jaws are librarians actively fighting to protect their budgets in "J.A.W.S."
- Islanders worried about preserving their tourism economy are librarians concerned with preserving their budgets.
- Mayor Vaughn represents not a group, but rather the complacent mind-set of those who are afraid of change and who wish to continue doing business as it has always been done.

The gist of the article is that while there are no great white sharks swimming around inside library buildings, there are predatory subscription prices lurking about and devouring poor defenseless budgets. The entire revised movie script can be summarized with this excerpt:

In Jaws, *police chief Brody exclaims:*	In "J.A.W.S.," *police chief Brody exclaims:*
"You're going to need a bigger boat."	"You're going to need a bigger library budget."

Even though *Jaws* depicts fictional events, the library nightmare version reflects a reality. The article encourages brave librarians to come together and defeat the rising-prices beast.

Do you see in your future using your creativity in or out of costume to get students interested in learning how to find and evaluate information? Do you have any ideas about unconventional approaches to the career that fellow librarians enjoy? Campus and community groups can develop a deep appreciation for the unconventional pirate librarian and the Second Life cybrarian as well.

Will you participate in Upward Bound programs and extend annual invitations to present to their students? Numerous campus groups at Notre Dame include their favorite cybrarian in their annual workshops as well. These workshops are for all age groups, but they trust that the material will be informative and engaging no matter how young the audiences. This generates positive evaluations for such workshops. Positive evaluations spread by word of mouth and lead directly to additional speaking invitations. When applying for promotions, these successes are clear demonstrations of your impact on the profession and the campus.

After reflecting on past workshop and publication successes, it seems logical that a future could involve drawing parallels between the futures of librarianship and yet another movie. Before deciding on a movie, the concept needs to be identified. This requires a literature review to find future trends or hot topics. The literature is focusing increasingly more on the next revolution, which will likely involve virtual schools of library and information science and e-science librarianship and what that means for the future of libraries. Information professionals are discussing e-science librarianship specifically as it relates to e-science and e-research and how to expand on the concept of the embedded librarian.

The literature discusses the progression of scientists moving from local, static, text data sets to more dynamic data sets globally. This suggests that there will be unforeseen challenges and opportunities for librarians to be trained—and, once trained, to organize and manage this new dynamic data. Basically, librarians are beginning to explore ways to form strong collaborations with e-scientists in an effort to ensure that they are involved in the planning stages of scientific projects using dynamic datasets or global resources. This partnership will allow for better data mining, retrieval, and preservation.

Just as a pirate theme immediately sprang to mind when teaching about the use of pirated material, and the theme of the movie *Jaws* seemed to perfectly compare to the tale of harmful subscription prices, yet another unexpected analogy emerged during the literature review for future trends. The best example to fit this comparison is not a movie about a high tech future with flying cars and holograms, but rather *The Lord of the Rings*. The next project will be "Lord of the e-Things: e-Science Librarian." The Lord of e-Things concept is a natural evolution from the pirate theme. This would allow one to dress like one of the characters in the trilogy, if it would be possible. It's all in the planning and uncommon creative vision.

When creating movie analogies, it is crucial to maintain focus on the main library points. One begins by highlighting needs, challenges, and opportunities for e-science librarianship, using an interesting analogy. If doomsday prophesies come true and libraries no longer house print material because artificial intelligence replaces human information retrievers, what will become of librarians? This reflects a similar tale of threatened annihilation, *The Lord of the Rings*. While there may not seem to be many obvious parallels between library science and the *Lord of the Rings* trilogy, a few characters are analogous to e-science librarians. For instance, there is a "fellowship between disparate people from distant lands who band together to accomplish a goal."

The world of Middle-Earth, a focal point of *The Lord of the Rings*, could inspire a focus on middleware, which is basically software that provides standard communication tools for knowledge sharing, collaboration, and interoperability between applications, computing resources, institutions and individuals, across cyber-infrastructure. Simply put, middleware assists global entities in connecting people to resources. The *Lord of the Rings* character Gandalf corresponds to the cyber-infrastructure, a magical entity that makes the journey possible. Oh, yes, and he gallantly battles and defeated the beast that was blocking progress.

Arguably, one of the main characters is an inanimate object, the magical and powerful Ring. This is not a normal ring. In this analogy, the main character is the data set, which is no ordinary data set. It is more dynamic and comes in different formats, not only text-based data. Different people call the Ring different names; for instance, Smeagol (Gollum) famously calls it "my Precious!" Large-scale scientific research conducted through distributed global collaborations enabled by the Internet is called "e-science." Some people use this "e-science" term while others use a broader term "e-research" but this scenario will use the former term.

Whatever you call it, Frodo Baggins is clearly the master of the Ring. In the world of e-science, naturally, the main characters are the scientists. They are the masters of the data. Nevertheless, there were times when Frodo needed help from his trustworthy sidekick Samwise Gamgee. At one point in the journey, Sam realizes that he could not carry the Ring, but he could carry Frodo. For the purposes of this scenario, Sam represents the embedded librarians who are along simply to support the endeavors of scientists. Librarians can't conduct the scientific research, but they can help the scientist reach their destination.

"Lord of the e-Things" refers to enterprising librarians who are not afraid to venture out of their safe, familiar surroundings (à la the Shire) to lead librarians on the journey of becoming the lord or master of this e-science trend. These adventurous souls will be positioned to lead libraries into the wonderful world of e-science and become the lords or masters of the future of e-science librarians.

With concentrated efforts, e-science librarians can provide these services for academia. The three main ingredients are data-skilled librarians, e-scientists, and adequate cyber-infrastructure. Combining these potent ingredients allow for tremendous possibilities. Who knows? Working together, these e-researchers may devise a new, single, universally accepted bibliographic format, or style guide. Regardless of the outcome, librarians and scientists across large distances will benefit from collaborating to provide long-term stewardship, access, and preservation and archival services to large-scale research data globally.

The future workshop would have to begin with the question "What is e-science?" The term is defined as "the process of facilitating access; disseminating and archiving e-research includes dynamic, multimedia data sets, not just static text data sets." E-research encompasses scholars in the humanities. Logically, e-science librarians would provide the same types of services for this new information. Colleagues are encouraged to "think as a librarian globally; act as a steward dynamically!" This is a chance to revolutionize librarians' roles for the next generation in the e-research era! For instance, the new role would transform librarians from perceived detached information gatekeepers into participating information processors.

A few in the vanguard of preparing for e-science services should be pointed out. These include but are not limited to Purdue University, CERN, Cornell University, the University of Illinois, Johns Hopkins University, the Woods Hole Oceanographic Institute, and Australia's Queensland University of Technology.

Naturally, the future workshop would feature planning requirements such as conducting a user-centered needs assessment and addressing concerns such as

- long-term archiving support.
- budget.
- finite capacity to infinity and beyond.
- large-scale cyber-infrastructure.

It should be noted that sharing resources across existing cyber-infrastructure would be time consuming and laborious.

Another topic would involve training. This unchartered level of service may require additional, intensive training for a different skill set to develop research data specialists, or e-science librarians. It would be interesting to survey library programs that offer any such training. Another challenge involves designating "yours, mine, and ours." While the possibility for international collaboration is ideal, this could quickly lead to ownership conflicts. Without appropriate planning, this has the potential to be an international workflow nightmare. It is crucial to clearly defined division of labor and responsibilities. Scientists, universities, or institutions need to agree on intellectual-property rights and cyber-security. Technical support, language barriers, and divergent library classification systems are all considerations as well.

Another opportunity is the chance to establish global, networked librarianship. Librarians currently cooperate with professional counterparts worldwide. This allows an opportunity to strengthen those relationships. Librarianship was traditionally structured around subject disciplines like the branch-library model. The Gen Xer in me, however, asserts that just because librarians have always done things this way doesn't mean we have to continue.

Summary of Existing and Potential Situations:

Old/Existing Condition	New E-Science Option
Subject divisions (branch-library model)	Multidisciplinary topics
Static text data	Dynamic, multimedia, visual data sets
Local, affiliated library patrons	Remote, foreign library users
Single, local scientific researchers	Multiple, global scientific research teams
Restrictive publisher license agreements	Open-access resources
Narrow, singular-focus scientific research	Heterogeneous, multidisciplinary research
Library-subject divisions, branch libraries	Interdisciplinary retrieval methods

This is a golden opportunity to maximize the future global Google-age generation of librarians for e-scientist services. Library and information science programs preparing students for roles as e-science librarians should have a competitive advantage.

If this e-science trend becomes a normal reality, librarians will need to find innovative methods to make their relevant services more visible and accessible to users. Whenever librarians provide a valuable service, outreach is always a vital need! Even if this e-science trend doesn't become the new norm, librarians need to continue taking a leadership role in creatively contributing to the university, the profession, and the community. They must continue to have a positive impact through instruction, outreach, and marketing initiatives. Keep in mind that promotional activities should not be confused with actual marketing. Promotions are the fun part of a marketing campaign. Marketing requires an inordinate amount of research, analysis, and planning. The following story points out the differences:

> If the circus is coming to town and you paint a sign stating "Circus Coming to the Fairground Saturday," that's advertising.
>
> If you put the sign on an elephant walking through town, that's promotion.
>
> If the elephant walks through the mayor's garden, that's publicity.
>
> If the mayor laughs about it, that's public relations.

If the residents go the circus, you show them the booths and answer questions, and they spend money, that's sales.

And if you planned the whole thing, well, now, that is marketing!

—*author unknown*

The way to become an extraordinary cybrarian is remarkably simple. The key is to find your passion and visualize methods for incorporating what you love to do into what you have to do. If you enjoy solving puzzles or word jumbles, create them for your classes or workshops. Chances are that the students will enjoy them also. The cybrarian became extraordinary as a result of revisions made based on user feedback. New active-learning exercises have the potential to be fun, but it is important to test them, evaluate them, and adjust them to effectively meet the desired learning goal.

If you enjoy using new technology, search professional literature to find out how others are using it in classes. It may be helpful to search general fields, not just libraries. Harvard University's CyberOne class would not have appeared in any library literature review. Nevertheless, the principal pedagogical premise would be adaptable for library instruction. Attending library or technology conferences or workshops should offer new ideas that can be modified to enhance library classes. If creativity is not a strong characteristic, simply adopt techniques to engage students that have been proven effective. Resist the urge to overwhelm the students with interesting activities. One small, well-timed mental break will do wonders for mandatory library-instruction classes.

The future of librarianship is what we imagine it to be in our wildest fantasy. The future of librarianship is what we challenge it to be and ultimately what we make of it. In summary, extraordinary cybrarians live to do that which has never been done.

The secret recipe for making an extraordinary cybrarian has three *F*s: failing, finding fun, and flying (technically that is four *F*s). Extraordinary cybrarians are not afraid to fail. For every article published, several others were rejected. Extraordinary cybrarians are not afraid to find fun new approaches to classes and publications. Last but definitely not least, extraordinary cybrarians are not afraid to fly—in Second Life or in real life!

APPENDIX A:
UPDATED STORYBOARD (PPT)

#1 -- Citation Cops

http://www.youtube.com/watch?v=eail-6fN_eg

Same amount of time if the announcer reads it or just show it long enough for people to read themselves. So I recommend letting the song play continuously

3-5 seconds

http://www.youtube.com/watch?v=eaji-6fN_eg

Same amount of time if the announcer reads it or just show it long enough for people to read themselves. So I recommend letting the song play continuously

3-5 seconds

#2 -- Graded Paper Shot

Frustrated Male student holding "F" graded paper surrounded by Style Manuals in a classroom setting

3 seconds

#3 -- Miranda Rights

Citation Cop (played by Bob L.) wearing RefWorks Hat slams down citation manual and says

"You have the right to Cite References easily and quickly!

You have the right to get A's on all of your Reference Citations!"

8 seconds

Citation Cop (played by Bob L.) holds up graded paper with "F"

You have the right to use RefWorks to cite your references automatically!

If you cannot afford RefWorks … it will be provided for you!

8 seconds (can use this alone instead of with the script above to reduce time)

Citation Cop displays RefWorks on Monitor

If you give up these rights any grades you get on Reference Citations can be used against you by the Dean of your College (or Academic Review Board?). Do you understand these rights?"

10 seconds

26 seconds for total script on this slide

#4 -- Ref-WHAT?

Student looks very confused and asks in exaggerated tone

"Ref Whaaat?"

2 seconds

#5 -- Moment of Clarity

Citation Cop places RefWorks Hat on the student's head and everything is clear!
The student exclaims:

"WHOA!

RefWorks…imports references automatically from databases; organizes and manages references and formats bibliographies in mere seconds!

COOL!"

14 seconds

#6 -- Lifesaver

Student removes RefWorks Hats and pulls out the same paper but the grade has magically changed to an even Bigger sized "A+" and the student celebrates:

"Thanks Citation DUDE!!
RefWorks …is a Lifesaver!"

10 seconds

#7 -- Citation Cops Closing Credits

http://www.youtube.com/watch?v=eail-6fN_eg

Closing scene from the 27 second point of YouTube clip to the end = 11 seconds

Or if only play the "Innocent until proven guilty in a court of law" excerpt = 7 seconds

APPENDIX B: JOURNAL HIGHLIGHTS AND EVALUATION SURVEY RESULTS

JJC JOURNAL HIGHLIGHTS

Year 2 ***Added the Kindles***

Day 1—Boys' B Pod

12 students; 2 were in my class last summer. So, while they were happy to see me, and excited about the new format using the Kindles, I was sad that they were back. Only 1 did not want to use the Kindle. I got the Kindles a few minutes before class; syllabus page numbers are different depending on font size.

All of the boys who used the Kindle loved it, especially the definitions when your cursor is near a word.

I didn't have time to get a student worker to help me with my JJC class, so I deputized proficient students. The 1 who didn't try it said he felt stupid because he doesn't know how to use electronic stuff. While others were writing, I showed him how to use it. He loved it, and actually showed me how to do something I didn't know how to do. I told him I'm proud of him. This is about teaching technical skills, no matter how small.

I only had 7; they had to share. I constantly heard screams of "I want to read!" "No, it is my turn to read!" Every librarian's fantasy has to be a classroom of kids fighting to read! Since an inmate choked a guard before I arrived, I didn't want a fight to break out, so I guaranteed that everyone would get a chance to use it.

The boy's favorite quote to discuss was Ralph Ellison's, the one in which he states, "I am invisible, understand, simply because people refuse to see me."

Day 3

1 student said he liked the activities but that he would rather we just read with the Kindles during the entire class. Guards had them write in their journals before class. That helped because the Kindles have reduced the journaling time. My scavenger hunt requires them to match people in the room with characteristics written on their papers. The correct person initials the paper. They figured out they

could save time by simply asking people, "Which one are you?" and then having them initial. That defeats the deductive-reasoning portion of the activity. But my real goal is to get them talking to each other, and they usually find out something interesting about a person they had not talked to before. I pretended to complain to the guards that they were cheating. The kids got a big kick out of outsmarting me. Even the guards teased me, saying, "They're in jail. Did you really think they would *not* cheat?"

Day 4

1 student told me he missed the start of class because he punched a wall to keep from punching a guard. Oh, OK, and I did notice his uniform changed colors to indicate he is violent. I noticed a second boy trying to, as he put it, "turn on the wireless." So I once again tried to explain that they cannot access the Internet on the Kindle. I could tell this student was trying, because he kept typing, and there was no need to type. After I wrestled the Kindle away, I noticed his uniform indicated a violent offender. Gulp! He is usually a good student and is a valuable contributor. I calmed down and considered that he may just be curious about other features. I told the guards I didn't want to get anybody in trouble. They said they couldn't replace the $400 device. I grew up in the 'hood, so I knew that "snitches get stitches." If I hadn't brought the Kindle, he would not be in trouble. After 3 hours with Amazon tech support, they replaced it for half price. I disinfected the others.

Day 5

I had to force the bullies to share. Are they seriously fighting over an electronic book? It's still a book!

They said the text-to-speech option would help people who can't read well. I hadn't considered that.

Day 6

16 final evaluations. I read the positive comments to reassure me that I am doing the right thing even though this pod was by far the most draining. I got two "I love you"s. They never flirted with me, so those were positively received. 1 student asked me if I had on perfume. "No," I replied. "That's Lysol on the Kindles." They all sniffed the cases and fell out laughing as I left the class. Girls are excited about seeing Kindles.

Group 2

Day 1—Boys' A Pod

Thrown for a loop—girls were reassigned, so I had another boys' pod. Are you kidding me? OK, calm down. The last class never tried to hit on me; they were like my babies, reminded me of my beloved nephews, and 1 had my nephew's weird nickname. 14 wonderful boys, who self-policed noise, insisted that 1 person speak at a time. Wow! 1 boy seemed very happy and upbeat, spoke and was very engaging, but was transferred to suicide-watch pod. Another reminder that I can't tell what they are dealing with.

Days 3–6 N/A

Bumped from the last 4 classes, so again no good-byes. I am actually getting used to being bumped.

Day 1—Girls' C Pod

14 girls, 2 from last summer. Since regular school begins next week, I will not have all six days. Teacher who blew me off sat in for 30 minutes because she'd heard good things about it. I invited her to join our discussion, but she said she didn't want to intrude. I showed her how to use the Kindle, and I rejoined the girls—and, yes, the guards, who were involved in a heated discussion. It was best that she blew me off. I may have been tempted to mimic her format. I was forced to do me. Vindication!

The girls' favorite quote for discussion was by an unknown author: "When the axe came into the forest, the trees said, 'The handle is one of us.'"

Day 2

1 student said she didn't feel comfortable writing down the answers on the Change Affirmation, even without putting names on the form and without turning them in. No mandatory parts of my class. I asked her to at least read the questions and think about the answers. I made a point to never ask their names, but I do notice what color Sharpie they use. She eventually wrote the most heart-breaking answers. I completely understand her resistance. She submitted the form, and I was amazed she shared that with me.

Day 3

This was a great class but was interrupted when a boys' pod erupted into a fight. Guards were running down the hall. 1 guard walked past holding ice on his bloody head. The boys didn't say a word to each other; they just walked up and started whaling on each other. Yet another reminder: This is real!

Day 4

10 final evaluations. The comments were once again all positive. One comment stated that she saw herself in one of the diaries and that before reading, she assumed she was the only one, but that opened her eyes. "And since that girl graduated and went to college, I can do it, too." That is why I do this.

KINDLE E-BOOK READER SURVEY RESULTS

56 Total Respondents

Age?

12 = 1
13 = 1
14 = 8
15 = 11
16 = 13

17 = 19
18 = 3

Grade in school?

6th = 1
7th = 2
8th = 1
Freshman = 12
Sophomore = 15
Junior = 12
Senior = 8

Do you prefer reading using the e-book reader?

Yes = 46
No = 10

Do you prefer reading the paper book?

Yes = 23
No = 33

Would you be MORE INTERESTED in reading if using the e-book?

Yes = 44
No = 10

Do you like using the e-book?

Yes = 50
No = 6

Like = ☺

Like a lil laptop
Smaller and won't need to mess with pages
It's electronic
Size and ability to store books
Easier to read
It is like a computer but it is not, it is a book
Easier to see the words
Can press the buttons to turn the pages
Can see the words better
New & grabs attention.
Same as a book
Get to look for pages
It's cool
Because it will be more fun

It's nice
Small and portable
It is better
Easier & interesting
Definitions
Carry lots of books in one
Everything
Easier to hold
It's digital
It keeps you interested
Love dictionaries, I always have one beside me but it's inconvenient

---

Dislike = ☹

Screen too small and seems to fade the words and makes it harder to read
Could give me light for I can see
If I drop it might break
Difficult to use
Paperback is easier
Too complicated

Do you or someone in your home own a laptop or computer?

Yes = 46
No = 10

Did you see your parents reading?

Yes = 46
No = 10

If yes, how often?

Always = 11
Often = 18
Sometimes = 17
Not at all = 3

Do you like to read?

Yes = 46
No = 10

If yes, how often?

Always = 17
Often = 14

Sometimes = 15
Not at all = 1

What would make you like reading more than you do?

Books that are movies
If I had an eBook I would read every minute if I could!
Having an eBook
Anything that grabs my attention.
I love reading!
Mysteries and griping stories
Interesting books
Free time on my hands
Money
If the book is thrilling and exciting
Staying in jail
Anything based on a true story
Non-fiction
Books I can relate to
If nothing else to do
Reading better

*************** Final Overall Surveys ***************

Do you like to read more as a result of this class?

18 = Yes
5 = No

Do you like to write more as a result of this class?

21 = Yes
2 = No

Do you like to discuss topics with people with different viewpoints more as a result of this class?

20 = Yes
3 = No

Are there any parts of this class that motivated you or will help you in your everyday life?

Some of the kids in the book is like me.
Read entry in book and it is exactly like me and I didn't realize that other people went through the same things. It opened my eyes but I'm not sure if I want to change yet. But I love this class because of the journals and writing.
By her bringing in these books/journals and us reading them made me feel like a Freedom Writer.

Even though I didn't go through as much as they did. But I still had fun with her doing the same stuff from the book.

When we read certain diaries and it hit real close to home.

It made me feel like I have hope. There's others out there that was in the ghetto that made it out.

Reading the book out loud and understanding everyone's point of view.

Not to judge anyone because there is a lot of people that are just alike and have similar problems.

The book motivated me, not really the class.

The book shows a lot of interesting points.

Yes, when we do activities and talk.

The e-reader

No because ain't nobody helping me get out of jail.

Maybe if it was an everyday class.

Yes it helped me become motivated.

Not really, sorry.

APPENDIX C: SAMPLE DAILY SYLLABUS AND WRITTEN CLASS ACTIVITY

SAMPLE DAILY SYLLABUS

Note: E-book pages are based on the largest font size.

Goals for this class are for students to

1. read critically.
2. write critically.
3. think critically.
4. use technology.

Icebreaker Activities

Kindles, journals, pens, and the *Freedom Writers Diary* books are distributed.

Write answers to Identity Chart in journals "What makes me unique?"

Write answers to "They Say ... I Say" in journals.

Read excerpts from the book using Wagon Wheel technique in circular seating arrangement.

Everyone reads at least one sentence using e-book reader.

p. 1, diary 1, "Ms. Gruwell." If interested, read a few sentences (e-book p. 208).

p. 23, diary 11, "Dyslexia." Read the first three paragraphs (e-book p. 516).

pp. 33–36, diaries 15 & 16, "Romeo & Juliet: Gang Rivalry" (e-book p. 648).

Journal Topics:

How do I see myself?

How do I believe others see me?

What makes me who I am?

How does the way we see ourselves affect how others see us?

What is my best characteristic?

What do I like most about who I am and the type of person I am?
Conduct a critical-thinking discussion based on journal entries.

WRITTEN CLASS ACTIVITY

(*Written exercise with greatest impact on JJC class)

MY CHANGE AFFIRMATION

I was _____
(Description of who you were)

I remember _____
(A sad memory)

I heard/saw _____
(Something you wish you hadn't)

I thought _____
(Where your life was headed)

BUT I WANT TO CHANGE

I am _____
(Accurate description of who you are)

I think_____
(How you perceive or see the world)

I plan to_____
(A goal you want to achieve)

I try_____
(Something you want to improve about yourself)

I feel_____
(Describe an emotion)

I forgive_____
(Someone who hurt you)

NOW I CAN CHANGE

I will _____
(Positive prediction of who will become)

I choose _____
(Something you want to do differently)

I dream _____
(Dare to dream big and bold thoughts!)

I hope _____
(Something you aim for)

I KNOW I WILL CHANGE FOR THE BETTER, STARTING NOW!

APPENDIX D: STALL NOTES

NECESSARY ROOM

It is impossible to lick your own elbow.
Yet everyone tries to when they learn that.

Look at the chart below and say the **COLOR** not the word

YELLOW ORANGE BLUE
BLACK **GREEN** RED
YELLOW PURPLE RED
ORANGE GREEN YELLOW

Did you know you can borrow laptops
from the Reserve Book Room for two hours?

Before you check out laptops, WASH YOUR HANDS.
Wash your hands with hot water for 10-15 seconds
that's long enough to sing "Happy Birthday."

PLEASE! LOOK... Before You Leave.
Make sure everything has flushed completely.

 Posting
approved by

UNIVERSITY OF
NOTRE DAME
University Libraries

---

iNFO 4 LiFe

Spring 2009

POSTING APPROVED BY HESBURGH LIBRARIES

Necessary Room Notes

A LIBRARY *FAIRY TALE*

Once upon a time in a far away land, lived a small leprechaun named Lil Scrappy who set out to find the perfect university. He traveled to a university called Xichigan. He had to get an article for class from the library located 500 miles across campus. He trudged through snow that was 8 feet high. Since he is only 2 feet tall he can't drive. He nearly froze to death trying to get to the article from the library. This made him very angry so he left.

He traveled to a university called South Xalifornia. Again his first assignment demanded that he walk 900 miles across campus to retrieve an article from the library. After a few days he finally reached the library. He climbed the 200 flights of stairs and found the journal. He used his last gold coin but the copier was broken. This made him really mad so he left for a new magical land that he saw drawn on the inside of the bottom of his empty pot of gold.

He traveled to a wondrous university called Notre Dame. For his first assigned reading his professor gave the class a link to the library's website for **"Electronic Reserves."**

Lil Scrappy was so excited that he was able to easily view the class reading directly online without going outside. Instead of being forced to go to the library he decided he wanted to visit this magical library to see this amazing place with powers equal to the greatest wizard. On his way he met a beautiful lady leprechaun named Iris Maximus. He got an "A;" fell in love; and lived happily ever after.

You don't need to be a powerful sorcerer to use Electronic Reserve; simply click on the link under Services located on the library's homepage.

INFORMATION FOR all aspects of LIFE
not just homework @ http://www.library.nd.edu

Fall 2009

Happy Halloween

Don't be afraid to Ask A Librarian.
We will use our powers to help you!

Necessary Room Notes

We can help you find scary movies in our collection, such as: Carrie, Exorcist, the Shining, Omen and Nightmare on Elm Street. We can help you find historical facts about *Halloween*. It goes back to the time when ancient Roman and Celtic festivals were combined. They began offering food, sacrifices and prayers to honor the dead. The Church named it *Halloween*. It changed the Roman Festival of the Dead from February to November 1st -- a Church holiday known as *All Saint's Day* or *All Hallows* because the term "hallows" means "holy people."

The evening before the holiday, October 31 became known as *All Hallows Eve,* and the church service performed on that evening was called All Hallowe'en.

 FIGHT THE FLU - WASH YOUR HANDS!

INFORMATION **FOR** all aspects of **LIFE**
not just homework @ http://www.library.nd.edu

 Hesburgh Libraries
University of Notre Dame

Posting Approved By Hesburgh Libraries

iNFO 4 LiFe

Fall 2009

Necessary Room Notes

TURKEY TALES

Fowl Mating Habits:
Studies by Schein & Hale revealed that male turkeys given a female turkey's head and neck on a stick will try to mate with that object the same as if it was a real female turkey (*see image*). A study by Carbaugh showed that male chickens responded best to models that actually had a female's body.

Eating Turkey Does Not Cause Sleepiness:

Scientists claim that L-tryptophan can only make people tired right away if it is consumed alone without any amino acids. The protein in turkey has plenty of amino acids. So instead of blaming turkey, nutrition experts explain that you may feel sleepy after your Thanksgiving meal because of all the carbohydrates you eat. Carbohydrates are in starchy & sugar-containing foods like breads, yams, potatoes, pumpkin pie, & other yummy desserts.

NEW! $1,000 Undergraduate Research Awards.
If you are doing research about turkeys or any other topic you could be one of **3 undergraduates** to **win $500** or **$1,000** from Hesburgh Libraries & the Center for Undergraduate Research. Go to
www.library.nd.edu/research-award/

FIGHT THE FLU WASH YOUR HANDS!

INFORMATION **FOR** all aspects of **LIFE**
not just homework @ **http://www.library.nd.edu**

 Hesburgh Libraries
University of Notre Dame
Posting Approved By Hesburgh Libraries

From *Cybrarian Extraordinaire: Compelling Information Literacy Instruction* by Felicia A. Smith. Santa Barbara, CA: Libraries Unlimited. Copyright © 2011.

INFO 4 LIFE

POSTING APPROVED BY HESBURGH LIBRARIES

Necessary Room Notes

 Why?

Top 3 Reasons Why Everyone Loves "Ask-a-Librarian":

3) Because you can pretend you have a personal research assistant when you schedule **appointments** with subject specialist librarians.

2) Because you do not think chatting online with a librarian, **until 1am,** is "creepy."

1) When you **chat online** with a librarian you don't worry about Chris Hansen's "To Catch a Predator."

Top 10 Reasons Why You Love Being an ND Student:

10. Because you are not afraid of getting "Schwinn-ed" *(run over by a bike).*
9. Two Words: Regis Philbin.
8. You read the du Lac: Student Handbook for fun.
7. You love Ramen Noodles & North Dining Hall pizzas.
6. Walking when the sidewalks are being watered is fun.
5. You never wanted to throw marshmallows at games.
4. You do not think Kegs & Eggs are nauseating.
3. You never get tired of hearing / saying "Go Irish!"
2. You cry every time you watch the movie, "Rudy."
1. You have an extra $49,000 for the next 4 years.

INFORMATION **FOR** all aspects of **LIFE**
not just homework @ http://www.library.nd.edu

iNFO 4 LiFe 4

Spring 2009

Necessary Room Notes

EASTER FUN FACTS

76% of Americans said chocolate bunnies should be eaten EARS first;

5% said bunnies should be eaten FEET first;

4% said eat the TAIL first.

90 MILLION chocolate bunnies are made yearly.

Do an online Easter Egg Hunt using the library's

NEW Catalog **Plus.**

Catalog Plus is a NEW service that can search the catalogs of Hesburgh Libraries, the Law Library, St. Mary's, Bethel, & Holy Cross *simultaneously.*

Catalog Plus asks "Did you **mean?**" -- Just like Google.

Catalog Plus lets you read & write reviews.

Catalog Plus lets you do much, much more.
Try it now @ http://www.library.nd.edu

iNFO 4 LiFe

POSTING APPROVED BY UNIVERSITY OF NOTRE DAME LIBRARIES

Necessary Room Notes

WHO YOU GONNA CALL? *Not Ghostbusters!*

Schedule Personal Research Consultation appointments using
ASK-A-LIBRARIAN
Ask a librarian questions either
by phone 631-6258, email, chat, or Instant Message (IM)

Q: Why did the chicken cross the road, north of ND Stadium?
  A: To go to the library.

Q: How many librarians does it take to change a light bulb?
  A: I don't know but I will be happy to look it up.

Q: What building on campus has the most stories?
  A: The library. Get it?

INFORMATION FOR all aspects of LIFE - -
not just homework @ http://www.library.nd.edu

 This is a holiday gift that all can share, Bathroom Etiquette Tips from *The Idiot Girls' Action-Adventure Club*.

This book introduces bathroom personalities. **Recognize anyone?**

TALKER: Is an easily identifiable chatterbox. Powers of this malefactor increase in strength once you're trapped in your stall. Once my stall door closes, "*SILENCIO!*" I'm a nameless entity. Don't attempt to talk to me. Don't ask me questions like, "*Boy! Spicy food again, huh?*"
> *Hint to Talkers*: "Hear me unzip, button your lip!"

TRESPASSER: Is one who invades the aroma & the audio space of an occupied stall by ignoring the "One-Stall Cushion" rule. Trespassers blatantly choose stalls next to you, despite available stalls further away from yours.

WAITER: Unlike the above, Waiters are not criminals; sadly they're just victims who are so polite that they choose not to do anything while others are present.
> *Hint to Waiters*: Courtesy flush for background noise, then release.

PRIMPER: Mortal enemy of the Waiter. If you cannot complete your prep work before leaving your house you forfeit your right to do so at any point in the day.

So a warning to all of you Trespassers, Talkers and Primpers: **BEWARE!**
Even if I don't see your face, I know your shoes!

To find this and other fascinating books, search ND's Catalog
@ http://www.library.nd.edu

Hint to Searchers:
If you want a **TITLE** that ND does not own, do an **INTERLIBRARY LOAN**.

Bathroom Etiquette: Verify That Everything Has Flushed
&
Fight the Flu Virus: Wash Your Hands!

 Posting approved by  UNIVERSITY OF NOTRE DAME University Libraries

From *Cybrarian Extraordinaire: Compelling Information Literacy Instruction* by Felicia A. Smith. Santa Barbara, CA: Libraries Unlimited. Copyright © 2011.

BIBLIOGRAPHY

Berkman Center for Internet and Society. "CyberOne: Teaching and Learning in Mixed Realities." http://cyber.law.harvard.edu/events/luncheon/2006/09/nesson/.

De Young, Raymond. "Stroop Task: A Test of Capacity to Direct Attention." http://www.snre.umich.edu/eplab/demos/st0/stroopdesc.html.

Dictionary.com. http://www.dictionary.com/.

Freedictionary.com. http://freedictionary.com/.

Gorby, G. L. "Use of Verbot Technology to Enhance Classroom Lecture." *Academic Medicine*, 76:5 (2001): 552–3.

Gruwell, Erin. *Freedom Writers: How a Teacher and 150 Teens Used Writing to Change Themselves and the World around Them.* New York: Broadway, 1999.

Gruwell, Erin. *The Freedom Writers Diary Teacher's Guide.* New York: Broadway, 2007.

Kane, Sally. "Generation X." http://legalcareers.about.com/od/practicetips/a/GenerationX.htm.

Jigsawsite. http://www.jigsawsite.com/.

New Line Cinema. *The Lord of the Rings*, directed by Peter Jackson. Burbank, Calif.: Warner Bros. Entertainment, 2001.

Robinson, Grant. Guess the Google. http://grant.robinson.name/projects/guess-the-google/.

Second Life. http://www.secondlife.com/.

Smith, Felicia A., "The Pirate-Teacher." *Journal of Academic Librarianship* 33:2 (2007): 276.

Stormfront. http://www.stormfront.org/.

Stormfront. Martin Luther King, Jr.: A True Historical Examination. http://www.martinlutherking.org/.

ThinkExist. Mark Twain Quotes. http://thinkexist.com/quotation/i-m_glad_i_did_it-partly_because_it_was_worth_it/166444.html.

ThinkExist. René Descartes Quotes. http://thinkexist.com/quotation/if_you_would_be_a_real_seeker_after_truth-it_is/223890.html.

ThinkExist. Ralph Ellison Quotes. http://thinkexist.com/quotation/i_am_invisible-understand-simply_because_people/223852.html.

Universal Studios. *Jaws.* Directed by Steven Spielberg. Hollywood, Calif.: Universal Studios, 1975.

Weusijana, Baba Kofi, Vanessa Svihla, Drue Gawel, and John Bransford. "MUVEs and Experiential Learning: Some Examples." *Innovate: Journal of Online Education* 5 (Jun-Jul 2009); http://www.innovateonline.info/index.php?view=article&id=702/.

Ziff Davis. http://www.pcmag.com/.

INDEX

About the Author

FELICIA A. SMITH, an associate librarian at the University of Notre Dame, is the librarian for sociology and Latino studies. Ms. Smith has published journal articles including "The Pirate-Teacher" and "Games for Teaching Information Literacy Skills" and contributed two chapters to *Librarians as Community Partners: An Outreach Handbook* (2009).